Damon H Albright

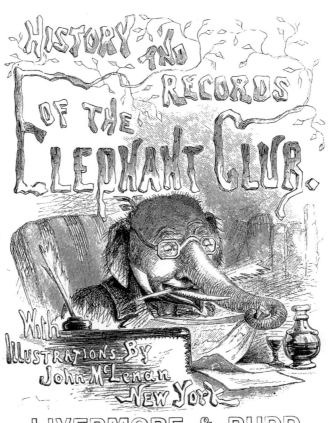

HISTORY AND RECORDS OF THE ELEPHANT CLUB.

With
Illustrations By
John McLenan
New York
LIVERMORE & RUDD.

The

HISTORY AND RECORDS

OF THE

ELEPHANT CLUB;

COMPILED FROM AUTHENTIC DOCUMENTS

NOW IN POSSESSION OF THE

Zoölogical Society.

BY

Knight Russ Ockside, M.D.,

AND

Q. K. Philander Doesticks, P.B.

NEW YORK:

Livermore & Rudd, Publishers,

310 Broadway,

1857.

W. H. TINSON, STEREOTYPER.

GEO. RUSSELL & CO., PRINTERS,
61 Beekman-Street, N. Y.

THIS IS THE VERITABLE AND VERACIOUS HISTORY OF THE DOINGS
AND MISDOINGS OF THE MEMBERS OF

THE ELEPHANT CLUB.

WITH A MINUTE AND PARTICULAR NARRATIVE OF WHAT THEY DID;
TO WHICH IS ADDED A COMPLEX AND ELABORATE DESCRIPTION OF WHAT THEY DIDN'T.

CONTAINING ALSO THE EXULTANT RECORD OF THEIR
MEMORABLE SUCCESS IN EVENTUALLY OBTAINING, EACH AND EVERY
ONE, A SIGHT OF THE ENTIRE AND UNADULTERATED

Animal,

FROM THE PRIMITIVE HAIR ON HIS ATTENUATED PROBOSCIS, TO THE
LAST KINK OF HIS SYMMETRICAL TAIL.

COMPILED

BY ME,

KNIGHT RUSS OCKSIDE, M.D.,

AND ME,

Q. K. PHILANDER DOESTICKS, P. B.

PREFACE.

---◆---

THIS book has been written by the Authors, and printed by the Publishers, in the hope that it may be purchased by the Public. If it proves to be a failure, the responsibility must rest with the People who don't buy it.

CONTENTS.

History and Records.

How They Met.

[Enter with a Flourish of Trumpets.]

SHAKESPEARE.

There were *no* two horses to be seen winding along the base of a precipitous hill; and there were *no* dark-looking riders on those horses which

11

were not to be seen; and it *wasn't* at the close of a
dusky autumn evening; and the setting sun *didn't*
gild, with his departing rays, the steep summit of the
mountain tops; and the gloomy cry of the owl was
not to be heard from the depths of a neighboring
forest—first, because there *wasn't* any neighboring
forest, and, second, because the owl was in better
business, having, some hours before, gone to bed, it
now being broad daylight. The mountain tops, the
lofty summits, the inaccessible precipices, the precipitous descents, the descending inaccessibilities, and
the usual quantity of insurmountable landscape,
which forms the stereotyped opening to popular
romances, is here omitted by particular request.

The time and place to which the unfortunate
reader's attention is particularly called, are four
o'clock of a melting afternoon in August, and a
labyrinth of bricks and mortar, yclept Gotham. The
majority of the inhabitants of the aforesaid place, at
the identical time herein referred to, were perspir-
ing; others were sweltering; still others were melting down into their boots, and the remainder were
dying from sun-stroke.

At this time, a young gentleman seated himself
behind the front window of the reading and smok-
ing-room of the Shanghae Hotel, in Broadway. The

chair he occupied was capacious, and had been contrived originally, by ingenious mechanics, for the
purpose of inducing laziness. The gentleman had
taken possession of this article of furniture for the
double purpose of resting himself from the fatigues
of a month's inactivity, and also securing a position
where he could see the ladies pass and repass, in
hopes that the sight might dispel the dull monotony
of a hotel life in the city, during summer. On this
occasion, to secure additional ease, the individual
had adopted the American attitude of raising his
feet to a level with his head, by placing them upon
a cast-iron fender behind the window—an attitude,
by the way, not particularly characterized by its
classic grace.

There was nothing remarkable in the dress of the
person to whom we have alluded. He was evidently
a victim to the popular insanity of conforming to
fashion. So strictly were his garments cut and
made in accordance with the prevailing style, no
one could doubt for a moment that the taste, or
want of taste, manifested in his dress, was not his
own, but the tailor's. In his hand he held a small
cane, with which he amused himself, first, by biting
the ivory head, then by making it turn summer-

saults through the fingers of his right hand, after the manner in which Hibernians are supposed to exercise their shillelahs.

Whether the activity in the streets, the appearance of the ladies with every variety of dress, or the gymnastic eccentricities of his cane, were particularly entertaining, is very questionable; certain it is, that the expression of his eyes showed gradually less and less of animation. By degrees his eyelids closed. His head soon vibrated with an irregular motion, until it found a support against the back of the chair. His hat fell from his head, and his cane dropped from his fingers. His muscles became fully relaxed. He was, undeniably, asleep.

He had been sleeping nearly a half hour, when an individual, who was walking leisurely down Broadway, casually glanced in the window of the Shanghae, where our first person singular was sleeping, with more seeming comfort than real elegance of position. He seemed struck with the appearance of the sleeper, and pausing for a brief time to survey his form, contorted, as it was, into all sorts of geometrical irregularities, curves, angles, and indescribable shapes, he entered the hotel, passed around into the room where the sleeper was, and did not stop until at his side. He again stood for a moment, silently contemplating the form and features of the sleep-bound stranger.

The second person was also singular. He was, apparently, about twenty-five years of age, with a full, florid, and expressive face. His body was quite rotund, even to corpulency; and, save a heavy moustache, his face was closely shaven. His clothes were of the thinnest material, and well adapted to secure comfort during the hot season. His expression, as he stood watching the first person singular, seemed full of doubt. At last, as if determined to remain in doubt no longer, he touched the somnolent first person lightly on the shoulder. First person singular opened his eyes with a spasmodic start, stared wildly about him for a moment, until his eyes rested upon the disturber of his slumbers.

"Excuse me, sir," said second person singular, "but an irresistible impulse led me to awaken you. The fact is, sir, a few years since, I had an intimate friend who was lost at sea, and such is the resemblance you bear to him, the thought struck me that you might be he. Were you ever lost at sea, sir?"

First person singular looked with some little astonishment upon his interrogator. He wiped the perspiration from his forehead, assumed an erect position in his chair, and replied :

" I don't think I ever was."

" It may have been your brother," said second person singular.

" It couldn't have been, for I never had a brother. By the way, I did have an uncle who, on one occasion, when hunting in Illinois, some fifteen years since, was lost on a prairie. Perhaps it's that circumstance to which you refer ? "

" No, it was at sea.   I'm sorry, sir, that I disturbed your sleep."

" You needn't be," was the reply, " for I went to sleep without intending to do so."

" Do you ever imbibe ?" was the next interrogation.

First person singular said he was guilty of no small vices, though he didn't care if he did take a brandy smash. The parties then adjourned to the inner temple of the Shanghae. Second person singular ordered the smash for his companion, and a sherry cobbler (so called from its supposed potency in patching up the human frame, when it is about falling to pieces under the influence of weather of a high temperature) for himself. A succession of singular coincidences followed. Each party suggested

at the same moment, that it was confoundedly hot
in the sun. Both simultaneously imbibed. Each
said he felt better after it, and each undoubtedly
told the truth. Both arose at the same instant,
inquired who the other was, whereupon two auto-
biographies were extemporized in brief. They disclosed the following facts. First person singular's
name was Myndert Van Dam; he was a descendent
of one of the Dutch families who originally colo-
nized Manhattan Island. He had been three years
absent in Europe, and on returning a few weeks
before, found most of his acquaintances had left the
city on account of the hot weather, and his experience had been one of uninterrupted dullness.
Second person singular rejoiced in the appellation of
John Spout. His genealogy was obscure, but so far
as he could learn, he was descended in a direct line
from his great grandfather on his mother's side. If
his ancestry had ever done anything which would
entitle their names to a place in history, it was very
certain that historians had failed to do their duty:
for he had never found the name of Spout recorded
in connection with great deeds, from the robbing of
a hen roost down to cowhiding a Congressman. He
was by profession an apothecary, and was laying off
for a few weeks' relaxation. Mr. Spout concluded

his personal narrative by suggesting the following proposition :

Whereas, We have demolished a smash, and annihilated a cobler ;

Resolved, That we now proceed to devastate a couple of segars.

Mr. Spout adopted the resolution unanimously, and by a further singular coincidence, they lighted their segars, and left the place for a promenade. A brisk rain beginning to fall, they sheltered themselves under an awning. A pair of gold spectacles containing a tall, sharp featured man, adorned with

an unshaven face and a brigandish hat, approached them, and asked Mr. Spout for a light. Mr. Spout acquiesced. The party in attempting to return the cigar, accidentally touched the lighted end to Mr. Spout's hand, and not only burned his hand slightly, but knocked the cigar out of the fingers of third party; whereupon, Mr. Spout extemporized a moderate swear. Third party apologized, and offered a cigar to Spout and Van Dam from his own cigarcase, which they accepted; and he hoped that in their future acquaintance, should they feel disposed to continue it, he would not again involuntarily burn their fingers. He announced himself to be Mr. Remington Dropper, a two years' importation from Cincinnati, and a book-keeper in the heavy hardware house of Steel, Banger & Co., down town.

"Mr. Dropper," said Spout, "I am happy to have made your acquaintance. My name is Spout—John Spout—chemist and apothecary, with Pound & Mixem, No. 34, opposite the whisky-shop. Allow me to make you acquainted with my old and valued friend Mr.—— Mr.—— what the devil did you say your name is?" said he, addressing Van Dam, aside.

"Myndert Van Dam," suggested the gentleman speaking for himself.

"Yes," resumed Spout, "Myndert Van Dam."

As they shook hands, Mr. Dropper's attention was called in another direction. He desired his companions to notice the fact that a man was approach-

ing with his umbrella, and having bought and lost too many articles of that description, he should not stand unmoved, and see the last one vanish from his sight.

An individual of small stature, apparently about forty-five years of age, with hair of an undeniable, though not an undyeable red approached, holding over his head a silk umbrella.

Mr. Dropper stepped forward and confronted him. He said he was aware that if every man were compelled to account for the possession of that which he claimed as his own, the world would hear some rich developments, in a moral point of view, respecting the tenure of property ; and it was precisely for this reason that he had stopped him in the street. He inquired of fat party with the silk umbrella, if he saw the point of his remark. Fat party confessed his inability to comprehend its intent. Mr. Dropper then proceeded to state that when he called fat party's attention to the subject of titles to property in general, he did suppose that fat party would be led to ask himself whether he had a legal and equitable title to the umbrella in particular which he was then under. Fat party fancied that he *did* perceive a lurking innuendo that he had stolen somebody's umbrella. Mr. Dropper was gratified to discover fat party's readiness of comprehension ; at his request fat party brought down the umbrella, which discovered the following words painted conspicuously on the cloth outside :

" STOLEN FROM R. DROPPER."

Mr. Dropper insisted that there was the evidence, " R. Dropper," meaning Remington Dropper—Remington Dropper being himself—" Stolen from R. Dropper," by whom ?—He would not assert positively

that fat party was a hall-thief, but he would say and
he did say, that his umbrella was found in fat party's
possession, without his permission. Some old stick-
in-the-mud had said somewhere, to somebody, sometime, that an honest confession was good for the
soul, and if fat party would acknowledge the unbuilt
whisky, he wouldn't appear against him on his trial
for petty larceny. Fat party repudiated the idea
that he was a thief. As far as Mr. Dropper's recollection assisted him he had always noticed that the
biggest rascals protested their innocence the most
emphatically. Fat party appealed to Mr. Dropper's
magnanimity to hear his explanation, which Mr.
Dropper consented to do.

The explanation developed the fact that fat party
was Mr. James George Boggs, late of the Department of the Interior, at Washington, who had
arrived that afternoon in the city with his sister,
Mrs. Banger, wife of Mr. Banger, of the firm of
Steel, Banger & Co., who, it is already stated, were
Mr. Dropper's employers. They went directly to
Mr. Banger's counting-room, and whilst there it commenced to rain; Mr. Banger offered Mr. Boggs
Dropper's umbrella to walk up with, Boggs accepted
it, and on his way up had been stopped on suspicion of theft.

Dropper made a humiliating apology, swore eternal friendship to Boggs, introduced him to Van Dam and Spout, and invited the party to his room to spoil a snifter from his private bottle. They accepted the invitation with commendable alacrity, and soon arrived at Mr. Dropper's cozy apartment, which was situated on one of the streets intersecting Broadway. At Mr. Dropper's request, they seated themselves in a circle around the table, with the view of calling up the spirits, but whether saintly or satanic, the compilers of these records do not venture an opinion. After sitting three minutes and twenty seconds in solemn silence, it was discovered that Dropper was a medium, as he was enabled to bring up the spirits in tangible and unmistaken shape from his closet, and forthwith communications of a very satisfactory character were made to the circle. Indeed, the opinion was very generally expressed, that the spirits were genuine spirits, and the medium an excellent test medium, through which they should delight, in future, to have further communications.

As they finished their wine a knock was heard at the door. Dropper responded with a "Come in." An Irish servant put her head within the apartment:

" Plase, sir," said she, "I have a caird here that

a gintleman at the door towld me to give to the red-headed gintleman as just come in."

Dropper viewed the card, and the four looked at each other for a moment, apparently with a view of discovering who it was that answered the description of a "red-headed gintleman." At last, Boggs spoke.

"I think it must be me," said he, receiving the card from Dropper, and reading aloud, from the back of it, as follows:

"Sir, an old acquaintance desires to see you for a moment, in relation to a matter involving your own interest."

"Show him up," said Dropper, "it will only make one more—that is, if Boggs is agreed."

Mr. Boggs had no objections to such course being taken, though he was deeply puzzled to know who the old acquaintance could be.

In a moment, the servant introduced into the room a tall, spare individual, of about thirty-two years of age. He was ordinarily attired, and, though not seedy, his garments were by no means new. His face was closely shaven, and surrounded by a large standing collar. He looked around the room upon the different parties present, until his eyes rested upon Boggs. He then ventured to speak.

"Gentlemen," said he, "excuse this interruption. The fact is, I have been seeking this gentleman for nearly three years past, and observing him in company with you, I could not forbear following to seek a brief interview."

Boggs turned pale. Visions of cowhides and pistols came before his mind.

"You are perfectly excusable," said Dropper, "We will leave the room, if you desire."

2

"N–n–not for all the world," ejaculated Boggs, hastily. "I have not the slightest objection to your remaining."

"Nor I," said the tall gentleman. "Your name," continued he, addressing Boggs, "is Johnson, I believe."

Nothing could have relieved Boggs from the suspense under which he was laboring more than this last remark. The gentleman had evidently mistaken him for one Johnson, who had, probably, insulted or injured the tall individual, on some previous occasion. The blush again returned to Boggs' cheeks.

"You are mistaken," said he, at last. "My name is Boggs."

"Boggs—so it is," said the tall stranger. "My bad memory often leads me into errors. But the mistake is very natural—Johnson sounds so much like Boggs; but, whether Johnson or Boggs, you are the individual whom I seek."

This announcement caused Boggs's courage to again descend into his boots.

"It is three years since I have seen you," said the tall individual. "During that length of time, a person would be likely to forget a name. But your person, sir, that I could never, never forget," continued the tall man, solemnly, and throwing in a little melo-dramatic action, as he spoke, which made Boggs shudder.

"C–c–certainly," said Boggs.

"Mr. Boggs," said the stranger, "you probably don't recollect me."

"C–can't say that I do," stammered Boggs.

"That need make no difference," said the stranger, mysteriously. "I know you."

The stranger then commenced feeling in his coat pockets with his hands.

Boggs sprang to his feet, observing this movement, fully satisfied that the stranger was seeking his revolver or bowie-knife.

"Sir," said Boggs, hurriedly, "if I have ever unconsciously done you an injury, I am ready to apologize. I can see no good reason why this apartment should be made the scene of a sanguinary conflict."

"Sanguinary conflict—apology"—said the other, somewhat astonished. "My dear sir, the apology is due to you."

Boggs's equanimity was once more restored. "You don't know how happy I am to hear you say so," said he. "Could you make it convenient to apologize at once, to fully relieve my mind of the frightful anticipations?"

"With the greatest pleasure in the world, Mr. Boggs," said the stranger. "I apologize."

"And I cheerfully forgive you," said Boggs.

"Then you recollect the circumstance, do you?" asked the stranger.

"Hang me if I do," said Boggs.

"Then you forgive me in anticipation."

"Certainly," replied Boggs. "But what the devil were you feeling in your pockets for so mysteriously?"

"My *porte-monnaie*," replied the stranger, who at length succeeded in finding the object of his search. He took from it a gold dollar, two dimes and a cent, and placed them on the table before Boggs. "There," said he, "is the sum of one dollar and twenty-one cents, United States currency, which amount is justly your due."

"What the deuce does all this mean?" asked Boggs, in his bewilderment; "for between being waylaid in the street, accused of petty larceny, anticipations of being murdered, receiving apologies for unknown injuries, and the proffer of money from a total stranger, I hardly know whether I am standing on my heels or my head."

The mysterious stranger then proceeded to make his explanation.

"About three years ago," said he, "I invited a lady friend to the theatre. She signified her intention to accept the invitation. In the evening I called for her, attired in my best, and found her seated in the parlor attired in *her* best. We arrived at the theatre. I had taken with me only a small sum of money—amounting in the aggregate to one dollar and thirty-seven and a half cents. I took the dollar from my pocket, and passed it to the ticket-seller, who took occasion to pass it to me again immediately, and putting his physiognomy before the seven by nine aperture through which the money goes in and the pasteboard comes out, he announced to me, in effect, that the bank note aforesaid, of the denomination of one dollar, was a base imitation. This was a perplexing position. Had I been the fortunate possessor of another dollar on the spot, I should not have been troubled. The lady's acquaintance I had but recently formed. My pride would not permit me to announce to her my true financial condition at that moment. Between pride and a hurried contemplation of the prospective frightful results of my monetary deficiency, I was completely bewildered. I stammered out something about having nothing with me except two or three shillings and a fifty dollar bill—the first of which, gentlemen, existed in the innermost recesses of my vest pocket, and the last in my imagination. I was wondering what the devil I should do next, when a gentleman with red hair addressed me. "Good evening, sir," said he, touching his hat, "did you say you have difficulty in getting a bill changed?" Without waiting for me to speak he said, "here's a dollar; you can return it to me to-morrow, when you call at my office to transact that matter of which we were speaking yesterday. Good evening." I looked in my hand, and found in it two half dollars and a card, upon which I perceived a name and address written. I was more bewildered than ever, owing to the unexpected deliverance, from what a moment before, I had believed to be an inextricable difficulty. I thought that heaven had deputed some red-haired angel to come to my relief. Then I doubted whether it was not a dream; but the weight of the two half dollars satisfied me that the whole thing was a tangible reality. The difficulty was dissipated, the funds were provided, and the necessary tickets purchased. Next morning I resolved to visit my deliverer, and give him my heartfelt thanks and a dollar. As I was about to leave on my joyful errand, I felt in my pocket for the card; it was gone. I was horror-stricken. I searched everywhere, but could not

find it. I tried then to recall to my mind the name;
but having read it under considerable excitement,
it had not impressed itself upon my memory. I
went to the theatre, in hopes to find it there, but in
vain. For three months, gentlemen, all my spare
time was employed in perambulating Broadway, and
standing at the entrance of the theatre, in hopes of
meeting my deliverer. Many are the short and red-
haired gentlemen whom I have vainly pursued. A
half hour since, as I was riding down Broadway in a
stage, I saw my deliverer turning the corner of this
street, in company with three other gentlemen. I
stopped the stage, gave the driver a quarter, and
without waiting to receive the change, I made a rush
for the stage door, stepped on the silk skirt of a lady
passenger, kicked a fat gentleman on the shins,
knocked a baby out of an Irishwoman's lap, fell, and
struck my head against the door, tumbled out, slipped on the Russ pavement, excited the mirth of the
passengers and pedestrians, got up, and reached the
corner just in time to see the party whom I followed
enter this house. I rushed on, and after some little
inquiry, succeeded in attaining this apartment.
Gentlemen, Boggs was my deliverer."

"Hurrah for Boggs," shouted Dropper.

"Boggs, you're a philanthropist," said Spout.

" *Vive le Boggs*," said Van Dam.

"Gentlemen," said Boggs, "I protest against your unwarranted compliments. My dear sir," said he, addressing the stranger, " you only borrowed a dollar of me, whereas, I perceive you have given me one dollar and twenty-one cents."

"Three years interest, at seven per cent," suggested the stranger, " Legally your due, and I insist upon your accepting interest as well as principal."

Boggs, without further objection pocketed the proffered amount.

" Your case," said Spout, to the stranger ; " is one of morbid concientiousness ; so much so that I feel desirous of knowing you better."

"My name, gentlemen," said the stranger, " is Dusenbury Quackenbush."

A general rush was made toward the stranger. Van Dam seized one hand, Boggs the other ; Spout caught him by the arm, whilst Dropper, who was the last to reach him, threw his long arms around the whole party. For a moment there was general commotion, growing out of a fierce shaking of hands and arms. Each person loudly assured Mr. Quackenbush of the happiness he felt in having formed his acquaintance. As soon as they had relieved him from their affectionate welcomings Mr. Quackenbush spoke.

"I am certainly happy to become acquainted with you, gentlemen," remarked he, "but really I am fearful I shall not be a very interesting acquaintance in a *coterie* of old friends, as you appear to be, and without doubt are."

"Yes, we are old friends," said Spout, "our friendship is as enduring as the gullibility of the public, and I might add as ancient as—as—gentlemen excuse me if I fail in this point to institute an appropriate comparison. As an astonisher, however, I will inform you of a fact known only to Mr. Van Dam and myself; and which is, that, two hours since, not one of the gentlemen of this quintet had ever known another of it; if I except the case of Mr. Boggs and Mr. Quackenbush."

"Mr. Quackenbush," inquired Spout, "allow me to ask whether you are acquainted with life in the metropolis in its multiform phases?"

"I confess my ignorance," was the reply. "It is most unfortunate that the position of a teacher in a public school is one not calculated to bring an individual in contact with much that is interesting."

"Taking that fact into consideration," said Spout, "I propose, that you all meet me at my room, two
2*

evenings hence, when I shall be prepared to unfold to you a purpose and a plan, which I have just conceived. My room, gentlemen, is over old Shavem's, the brokers, three doors from the corner. The number would be 461½, if there were any on the door. You can't mistake the place, however; there is an antiquated pump in front, and when I'm at home there is a Spout inside."

" Oh—h !" groaned Dropper.

" Never mind," resumed Spout, "I don't often attempt such things. Can I depend upon your coming ?"

All gave an affirmative response.

"Then," said Spout, "you can depend upon my going, I pronounce this meeting adjourned."

After a few words the parties separated.

How The Club Organized.

Put out the light, and then put.—SHAKSPEARE.

He evening arrived on which the gentlemen, named in the last chapter, were to meet in the
room of Mr. John Spout.

85

Mr. Spout was there, awaiting the arrival of his friends. He was seated at the end of a table, in a large easy-chair, in his dressing-gown. Before him, on the table, were several written papers. The apartment was one of moderate dimensions, neatly carpeted, and, with plenty of furniture, unobjectionable in quality and taste. On the walls were suspended various pictures, engravings, fencing-foils, and masks, boxing-gloves, antique models, Indian ornaments, plaster casts of legs, arms, hands, feet, &c. On either side of the table were two chairs, placed there, evidently, in anticipation of the arrival of his friends.

Several pipe-stems protruded from a pasteboard box, which was on the table. It required no unusual shrewdness to guess at the contents, and to rightly determine that it was filled with the best-abused, and, at the same time, best-used weed known.

One by one, the other gentlemen arrived, and were ushered by the housekeeper into Mr. Spout's apartment. They sat, engaged in discussing tobacco and the events of the day. At length, Mr. Dropper inquired of Mr. Spout if he had as yet fully elaborated the idea which, on the occasion of the previous meeting, had seemed to weigh so heavily on his mind?

"I was about to advert to the subject," said Mr.

Spout. "It has engaged my undivided attention up to the present time, and the idea and plan based upon it are sufficiently perfected to satisfy myself."

"Trot it out," said Boggs, "we are all attention."

"The fact, gentlemen," said Spout, "that most of our number have been either absent from the city, or so much engaged in our different vocations that we have never gained, or have lost, familiarity with many interesting phases of life, as it exists in New York, suggested to me the thought of devoting some portion of our time to looking about, and having put our observations in writing, to interchange them for our mutual gratification."

"A capital idea," said Mr. Dusenbury Quackenbush.

"Brilliant with pleasurable results," remarked Mr. Myndert Van Dam.

"Replete with rational enjoyment," suggested Mr. Remington Dropper.

"I'm in," was the laconic response of Mr. James George Boggs.

"Then I suppose I can count upon your coöperation in the realization of the idea," said Spout.

A general affirmative answer being given, Mr. Spout continued.

"You being unanimous," said he, "I'll now proceed to unfold my plans. To secure unanimity of action and entire success, it is necessary that we have a plan of organization. But in thinking upon this subject, I have foreseen that, by the adoption of any of the ordinary plans, we saddle ourselves with a useless machinery, which will hinder the successful accomplishment of the object we desire. We have no time to spare in discussing rules of order, the adoption of which invariably makes disorder the rule. Yet, there must be a head. In brief, then, gentlemen, I propose that the principles upon which our meetings shall be governed, shall be a despotic principle, but one which shall be compatible with the largest liberty of the governed. How do you like the idea?"

"The idea looks paradoxical to me," said Van Dam.

"Rather profound," suggested Quackenbush.

"Funny," said Boggs.

"I can tell better when I hear the rules," said Dropper.

"I have them prepared," continued Spout. "Shall I read them to you?"

"By all means," replied Van Dam.

The others signified an affirmative response.

Mr. Spout then proceeded to read :—

"We, whose signatures are hereunto affixed, do hereby organize ourselves into a club, having for its

NAME,

THE ELEPHANT CLUB, and having in view the following

OBJECTS:

1. The enjoyment and amusement of its members through.

2. A profound study of the Metropolitan Elephant, by surveying him in all his majesty of proportion, by tracing him to his secret haunts, and observing his habits, both in his wild and domestic state.

OFFICER.

"The only officer of the club shall be a High-oldboy, whose

DUTY

It shall be to sit in a big chair, at the end of the table, and to see that the members conform to the following

RULES OF CONDUCT:

1. In the meetings of the club, every member shall do exactly as he pleases.

2. Each member shall speak when he pleases, what he pleases, and as long as he pleases.

N. B.—If the remarks of any member are particularly stupid or tedious, the other members are under no obligations to remain and hear them.

" N. particular B. Should the speaker, at the conclusion of his remarks, find himself in the presence of only a part of his original audience, and some of those asleep; he is at full liberty, for his private satisfaction, to conclude that his eloquence, like that of the traditional parsons, is not only moving and soothing, as evidenced by the absence of some and the somnolence of others, but so satisfactory that those who were awake will never care to hear him again.

3. No member shall be permitted to bring spirituous or fermented liquors, wine, beer, or cider, whether imported or domestic, into any of the meetings of the club, under the penalty of passing them around for general use; unless the member prefers to keep them to himself, from motives of economy—the economy in such case to be regarded as an offence, to be punished with a severe letting alone.

4. The third rule shall apply to cigars, cheroots, and cigaretts.

5. Ditto — ditto — sardines, Bologna sausages, crackers and cheese.

6. Members are prohibited from sitting with their feet on the table, unless in that position they sit with more comfort, or they have other reasons satisfactory to themselves.

N. B.—The Higholdboy, in consideration of his onerous duties, is exempted from the action of this rule.

7. The Higholdboy is empowered to reprimand any member, when he considers it necessary to preserve the dignity of the club.

N. special and particular B. In order that this rule shall not operate prejudicially to the sovereign rights of individuals, the members of the club are at liberty to treat the reprimand of the Higholdboy as a good joke.

8. Any member who shall be absent from any meeting of the club, shall be liable to stand a half-dozen on the half shell for each of his fellow-members, unless he gives *no* previous notice to the club, or any member thereof, of his prospective absence. Such notice, which he fails to give, to be either verbal or written, at his own option.

9. These foregoing rules shall in all cases be construed strictly, they shall never be repealed or

amended; and shall be of binding force, except as hereinafter provided in the

ORDER OF BUSINESS.

1. The Higholdboy shall announce the suspension of all rules for three months.

At the conclusion, Mr. Spout, in a solemn tone, addressed the party.

"Gentleman," said he, "I am aware that the rules, which I have prepared and submitted, are stringent in the extreme, but I think they will be found, on examination, to be no more so than is essential to secure that unanimity of action so indispensable to the accomplishment of any great end. Believing, then, that you fully appreciate the importance of the end we have in view, I trust they will meet with your approval. Gentlemen, I give way to others."

Mr. Spout took his seat, amid manifestations of the approval of his associates.

Mr. Boggs was the first to speak on the subject of the rules.

"Gentlemen," said he, "unaccustomed as I am to public speaking, and overpowered as I feel at the present moment, I should do injustice to my own

feelings, did I fail to endorse the excellence of the rules reported by my friend Spout, and to give my unqualified adhesion, in accordance with the spirit which pervades them."

Mr. Dropper said that he had but one fault to find. He was by nature fond of resisting all rules, the idea of which he had always associated with a restriction of individual liberty. The rules proposed by Mr. Spout contemplated no restriction. They were so nice an adjustment of the relations between the governor and the governed that he could not find it in his heart to resist them. Hence he would be debarred his usual gratification of combatting them. Still he was willing to give them a trial.

Mr. Quackenbush liked the rules very much, as he thought it was coming down to first principles.

Mr. Van Dam said that, so far as he was concerned, the matter was all right; if it wasn't, "he'd make it right."

An inquiry was made as to who would fill the office of the Higholdboy.

Mr. Spout replied. He said that their club was an anomaly. It differed in its features from any organization which had ever been made. He thought that its individual peculiarities should be kept up in the matter of the election of its presiding officers. He was in favor of self-elevation to the position, and of letting the voluntary acquiescence of the members measure the duration of individuals' tenure of office—in other words, when they got tired of him, leave him to preside over a meeting composed of himself and the furniture. "Now, gentlemen," concluded Mr. Spout, "who wants to be a Higholdboy? Don't all speak at once."

Van Dam looked at Boggs; Boggs glanced at Dropper; Dropper eyed Quackenbush, and Quackenbush turned his eyes upon Spout.

"No one speaks," said Spout, "which leads me to believe that no one desires the position unless it be myself, which I confess, gentlemen, is true. Gentlemen, I declare myself duly elevated and installed into the office of Higholdboy of the Elephant Club, and when you survey my proportions, and look at the size of that chair, I am satisfied you will concede that I am well adapted to fill it. In conclusion, gentlemen, I ask of you your coöperation in forwarding the aims and purposes of this club. Mr. Boggs, will you pass me the tobacco-box?"

"Certainly," said Boggs, as he passed the box, "and allow me to congratulate your constituency in having elevated you to so responsible a position."

"A very respectable constituency of one—Spout," said Mr. Quackenbush. "But it is very funny, isn't it?" said he.

"It's a go," said Dropper.

Mr. Van Dam was very glad that he wasn't the lucky man, as he had such an abhorrence of responsibility.

The question of the time and place of meetings was the next subject discussed. It was finally agreed to leave that matter for future consideration.

"Gentlemen," said Spout, "I have assumed a responsibility, in anticipation of my attaining the Higholdboyship of this club. In this, perhaps, my course will not meet with your full approval; the nature of the step you will be apprised of in the room below. Will you accompany me?"

The party assented, wondering what further surprise was to greet them. They entered a rear parlor on the first floor, where an excellent dinner was waiting them, got up at the expense of Mr. John Spout, Higholdboy of the Elephant Club.

A good dinner is an excellent ending for any thing—even a chapter.

The Elephantine Den.

Off with his head so much.—SHAKSPEARE.

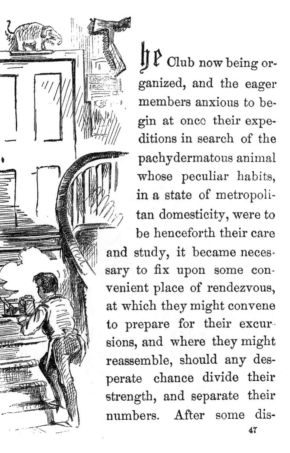

h e Club now being organized, and the eager members anxious to begin at once their expeditions in search of the pachydermatous animal whose peculiar habits, in a state of metropolitan domesticity, were to be henceforth their care and study, it became necessary to fix upon some convenient place of rendezvous, at which they might convene to prepare for their excursions, and where they might reassemble, should any desperate chance divide their strength, and separate their numbers. After some dis-

cussion as to the most convenient locality, a room in
Broadway was selected, as being less likely to attract
attention if lighted up and showing signs of occu-
pancy at an unseasonable hour; and as being easily
accessible in case a member was compelled to evade

the pursuit of an avenging M. P.; or should he be
taken suddenly drunk, and stand in need of brotherly
assistance.   It was not on the first floor, lest it should
be mistaken for a tavern; nor on the second, lest the
uninvited public should stray up stairs, thinking it
to be a billiard saloon; neither was it in the attic, as
the gas didn't run so high; but on the third floor

of an imposing building, a room was discovered, appropriate in dimensions, convenient in locality, and the rent of which was not so high but that its altitude was easily admeasured by a weekly V. It is not our present intention to designate the identical numeral which, in the directory, would point out the precise latitude of this mysterious apartment to the anxious inquirer. Suffice it to say that it was in the immediate vicinity of the public office of the man whose name is synonymous with that of the adolescent offspring of the bird whose unmelodious note once saved the imperial city from its fierce invaders, and that the occupation of this man of the ornithological appellation is to provide food and drink for hungry humanity. The relative situations of the club-room and this restaurant were such, that a plummet, dropped from the chair of the Higholdboy, would, if unimpeded by interposing floors, fall directly upon the private bottle of the amiable proprietor in the bar below.

By the timely suggestion of Mr. Remington Dropper, ingenious advantage was taken of the proximity of an establishment so praiseworthy, and so conducive to the common comfort. A wire was arranged, running from a point ever in reach of the chair of the august presiding officer, thence to a bell in

3

the room beneath. A system of tintinabulatory sig-
nals was contrived, that the dispenser of good things,
on the first floor, might be made to comprehend the
wants of the thirsty individuals in the loft, without
their coming down stairs. One jerk meant " brandy
smashes" all round; two pulls signified " hot whisky
punches, with plenty of lemon ;" a prolonged jingle
was to be immediately answered by an unlimited
supply of ale, porter and pewter mugs; while a convulsive twitch, or a couple of spasmodic tugs, signified to the man in waiting, not only that the entire
club was "over the bay," but that they wanted, on
the instant, soda-water enough to float them in safety
to the shore again.

The furniture of this private elephantine den was
simple, but necessary, made not for ornament, so
much as contrived for use, and consisted of a long
table, with an extra quantity of super-solid legs, in
case the club should all take a freak to go to bed on
it at once—two chairs for each member, one for the
customary use, and the other for the accommodation
of his feet, an upright piano-forte, a huge match-
box, and a wash-tub for empty bottles. A journal
was also provided, in which to inscribe the proceedings of each evening, and, by general agreement, it
was made a standing order that no man should write

therein unless he was sufficiently sober to tell a gold pen from a boot-jack.

The poker was chained to the grate, that it might not, in case of an unusual excitement, become a convenient instrument for the demolition of furniture, or the extinguishment of an offending member. For the same reason, the water-jug was tied to the door-knob, and the private tumbler of each member made fast to one of his chairs with an elastic band, so that, should he throw it at any one, he would not only miss the object of his unnoble aim, but the elasticity of the securing thong would cause it to recoil upon his own pate, with a force which would, probably, render him for the future less inclined to experiment in projectiles. Over the entrance-door, on the outside, was placed a toy elephant, two feet long, but four feet underneath, imported from Germany, at the unheard-of cost of ten dollars.

The room being furnished, and the club ready to commence operations, it was deemed expedient to select an individual of superior physical strength to attend to the door, lest some intruding outsider might sometime interrupt the deliberations of the honorable quadrupedal order. Mr. Quackenbush elected himself to this dignified and honorable office, and, under the belief that his brawny arms were eminently suited to do duty in case of the irruption of sacrilegious outsiders upon the sanctified premises, all the other members acquiesced in his promotion. If any undesirable person presented himself for admission, he was to inform him of the secrecy of the convention. Should the outsider persevere, he was first to expostulate with him, and endeavor to persuade him to go peaceably away. If all milder means should prove unavailing, he was first to black both of his eyes with a pewter mug, taking care to do it impartially and symmetrically, that the discoloration of one optic should not in the least exceed that of the other; he was then mildly to knock him down with a chair, pitch him gently, head first, down both flights of stairs into the street, and then, having filled his boots full of gravel, and put a brick in his mouth, he was to leave him; but on no account was he to deal harshly with such offender, unless he chose to do so on his own responsibility, or was specially authorized by a unanimous vote of all the members awake, in which case he might act his own pleasure. He solemnly bound himself, in case he should at any time be overcome by fatigue, or any other potent cause, that he would go to sleep immediately before the threshold, in order to prevent any animated worldling from penetrating into the secret den, and spy out the mystic doings of the elephants, without forcing an entrance over his prostrate body.

The arrangements being now complete, a solemn convocation of the honorable body was held, and a quadrupedal quorum being present, after a smoky and juicy deliberation of some seven hours, the Highold-boy, Mr. John Spout, unanimously *Resolved:*

1. That the club proceed to hunt the long-nosed animal.

2. In a body.

3. To-morrow night.

To this series of resolutions each of the other members acceded.   The result of this bold determination will be fully detailed in another chapter.

First Discoveries of the Club.

"He who fights and runs away,
Will live—"

A. NONYMOUS.

PURSUANT to the resolutions unanimously adopted on the evening before, the Elephant Club met to proceed, under the direction of some experienced hunter, to scrutinize their ponderous game. Being duly equipped with all the arms and ammunition required for an expedition of so perilous a nature, they sallied forth. They dragged no heavy, ponderous artillery, they wore no clanking swords, they rallied under no silken banner, and marched to no inspiriting music; but they tramped along, their only rallying-flag being a yellow handkerchief round the hat of Mr. Myndert Van Dam, who had thus protected his "Cady" from any injury from a sudden shower; their only martial music was the shrill pipe of Mr. James George Boggs, who whistled "Pop goes the Weasel," and for arms each one had a hickory cane, and in the breast

pocket of his overcoat, a single "pocket-pistol,"
loaded, but not dangerous. Mr. Remington Dropper
had assumed the leadership, and was to conduct the
party on their cruise.

They had proceeded but a short distance when
Mr. Boggs called out to the party to observe the
motions of a queer-looking character, who was
approaching at a distance of a half block. He was
stepping on the edge of the side-walk with his gaze
fixed upon the gutter, and in apparent uncon-
sciousness of the existence of anything but himself.

He was lank, lean, and sallow. His clothes were quite dilapidated, his beard and hair long. A smile on his face seemed to indicate his entire satisfaction with himself. He was a marked character, and after a moment's sight at the individual, inquiries were made of Mr. Boggs as to who he was.

"That is more than I can say," was Boggs's response. "I have known him by sight for years, and he has always appeared the same. He belongs to a class of beings in New York, a few specimens of which are familiar to those who frequent the principal thoroughfares, and are known by the ornithological appellation of " gutter-snipes." I have often talked with him, but he knows nothing of his own history; or, if he does, chooses not to reveal it. He is a monomaniac, but perfectly harmless, and calls himself Nicholas Quail. I have learned from other sources a few facts of his history. He sleeps anywhere and everywhere, and eats in the same localities. Nobody ever harms him, all being familiar with his whims. As far as I can learn, he was formerly a raftsman. He has never in his life owned real estate enough to form the site for a hen-coop, nor timber sufficient to build it. His personal property could be crowded into a small pocket-handkerchief; but let him get four inches of whisky in him, and he fancies he has such boundless and illimitable wealth, that in comparison,

the treasures of Aladdin, provided by the accommodating slave of the lamp, would be but small
change. He walks about the streets viewing what
he terms the improvements he is making; he gives
all sorts of absurd directions to workmen as to how
he desires the work to be done, much to their amusement. But here he is, now; if he is tight we'll have
some sport."

As the personage approached, Boggs accosted him,
when the following dialogue took place.

"So Nicholas," said Boggs, "you've come back,
have you? How is the financial department at
present ?"

Nick looked up and smiled.

"The fact is," said he, "I've just been buying
all the grain in Michigan, Wisconsin, Ohio, and
Indiana for $7 a bushel, and I am rather short for
small change, but if you want a hundred thousand
or so, just send a cart round to my office. Would
you prefer having it in quarter eagles or twenty
dollar pieces ?"

"Well, Nick, I don't care to borrow at present,
but a boy says you've been drunk. How is it ?"

" What boy is it ?"

" Your boy in your counting-room—the urchin
who runs on errands for you, smokes your stubs, and
pockets the small change."

" Now, hadn't he ought to be ashamed of himself, the red-haired devil, for getting Old Nick into such a scrape by his drunken lies ? Haven't I made him presents enough ? It was only last week that I gave him a house in Thirty-second street, and a splendid mansion on the North River ; and on the 4th of July he had fourteen thousand dollars, all in pennies, to bûy fire-crackers and soda-water with ; and yet he goes to you and lies, and says that I've been drunk. Don't you believe the lying cub ; he's got a spite agin me, because last night I wouldn't give him the Erie Railroad to bet on poker ; but I couldn't do it, General ; I seen the cards was agin him ; the other feller held four kings, and he hadn't nothin' in the world but three high-heeled jacks and a pair of fours."

" I do believe you were drunk," said Boggs, " and if you ever get hauled up before the justice you will have to pay ten dollars, and if you have not that decimal amount handy, you had better entrust it to the boy's keeping, to have it ready in case of such an emergency."

Nick felt in his pockets, and with a puzzled air remarked :

" I haven't got the money here, but I'll give you a check on the Nassau Bank for a thousand, and you can give me the change ; or I'll give you a deed of Stewart's, or a mortgage lien on the Astor House."

"Shan't do it, shan't do it, Old Nick; and I'm afraid you'll have to go to Blackwell's Island, sure."

"There's that infernal island again," said Nick; "if I'd ever thought it would come to this, I never'd have given that little piece of property to the city; but I'll buy it back next week, and use it hereafter for a cabbage garden; see if I don't."

By this time the Elephants seemed to disposed to go, but Nick spied on the shirt-front of Mr. John Spout a diamond pin, which seemed to take his fancy. He offered in vain a block of stores in Pearl street, the Custom-House, the Assay-Office, the Metropolitan Hotel and three-quarters of the steamer Atlantic, and to throw into the bargain Staten Island and Brooklyn City; but it was no use, the party took their leave, and Nick was disconsolate.

Passing up Broadway, their attention was attracted by one of those full-length basswood statues of impossible-looking men, holding an impracticable pistol in his hand, at an angle which never could be achieved by a live man with the usual allowance of bones, but which defiant figure was evidently intended to be suggestive of a shooting-gallery in the rear.

Mr. John Spout, who was in a philosophic mood, re-marked that it was a curious study to observe the various abortive efforts of aspiring carpenters to represent the human form divine, in the three-cornered wooden men, which stand for "pistol-galleries;" and the inexplicable Turks, the unheard of Scotchmen, and the Indians of every possible and impossible tribe, which are supposed to hint "tobacco and cigars."

The ambitious carpenter first hews out a distorted caricature of a man, which he passes over to the painters to be embellished. By the time the figure has survived the last operation, it might certainly be worshipped without transgressing any scriptural injunction, for it certainly looks like nothing in " the heavens above, the earth below, or the waters under the earth." It is, however, an easy matter to distinguish the Highlanders from the Turks, by the fact, that the calves of their legs are larger around than their waists, and they are dressed in petticoats and plaid stockings; the Turks and Indians, however, being of the same color, might easily be confounded, were it not for the inexplicable circumstance that the former are always squatting down, while the latter are invariably standing up; they are all, however, remarkable for the unstable material of which their countenances are manufactured; after one has been exposed to the boys and the weather for about a fortnight, his nose will disappear, his lips come up a minus quantity, the top of his head be knocked off, and a minute's scrutiny will generally disclose the presence of innumerable gimlet-holes in his eyes. The boys, in their desire to comprehend perfectly the internal economy of these human libels, not unfrequently carry their anatomical investigations to the extent of cutting off a leg or two, and amputating one or more arms, or cutting out three or four ribs with a buck-saw or a broad-axe. Indeed, there is one unfortunate wooden Indian, of some fossil and unknown tribe, on exibition in front of a snuff-shop in the Bowery, who has not only lost both legs, one arm, and his stomach, but has actually endured the amputation of the head and neck, and bears a staff stuck in the hole where his spine ought to be, and upon a flag is inscribed the heartless sentence, " Mrs. Miller's Fine Cut—for particulars inquire within."

Mr. John Spout having concluded his explanatory remarks, the entire party went into the pistol-gallery before-mentioned, to have a crack at the iron man, with the pipe in his mouth.

The nature of Mr. Quackenbush's profession, that of a teacher, was not such as would make him familiar with the use of fire-arms, and, in point of fact, he had about as good a notion of pistol-shooting as a stage-horse has of hunting wild bees; but he resolved to try his hand with the rest. When it came to his turn to try, he spilled the priming, and fired the hair-trigger instrument, accidentally, four times, to the imminent danger of the bystanders, before he could be taught to hold it so that it wouldn't go off before he got ready. He finally got a fair shot, and succeeded in breaking a window immediately behind him, after which he concluded he would not shoot any more.

As the other side of the room was used for a bowl-ing alley, the company proceeded to have a game of ten-pins ; and here, again, Mr. Quackenbush distin-guished himself. After dropping one ball on his toes, and allowing another to fall into a spittoon, he succeeded in getting one to roll down the alley ; with his second ball, by some miraculous chance, he got a "ten-strike," knocking down, not only all the pins, but also the luckless youth who presided over the setting-up-department.

Having refreshed themselves, the party once more regained Broadway, and consulted as to what place should be visited next.

Mr. Spout suggested that he would like to smoke. Nobody dissented except Mr. Dropper, who said he had read the day previous, in the morning papers, that a Turkish elephant had arrived in town, and was on exhibition on Broadway, above the Metropolitan Hotel. Thinking that a comparison instituted between the Turkish quadruped and the one which it was their particular office to study, might be of benefit to the members of the club, in their investigations, Mr. Dropper suggested that the smoking be dispensed with, until they should come into the presence of the oriental animal. Onward the zoölogical specialists sped their way, sometimes marching in Indian file, and sometimes arm-in-arm, running over little boys, dirty dogs, dry-goods boxes, low awnings and area railings, until at last Mr. Dropper cried " Halt !" before the portals of the den wherein the mysterious elephant, which had arrived from Constantinople, was concealed. It became a question who should lead in making an entrance. Boggs was fearful, Van Dam was afraid, Spout was cautious, Quackenbush would a little rather not, but Dropper's courage failed not, and he walked boldly into the outer temple, followed by his timid associates. Here they discovered a long counter, and a glass show-case, in which were displayed queer shoes, quaint tooth-picks, funny pipes, and singular ornaments. A glass jar, filled with a rose-pink fluid was also on the counter. A tall gentleman with a ferocious moustache, and a diminutive red cap, without a front-piece, met them. Mr. Quackenbush's curiosity was in a single direction; he said he wanted to go through the harem. They finally entered into the rear apartment. Here their wondering eyes beheld a long room, well lighted with gas. In the centre was a small basin, in which goldfish were indulging in their accustomed aquatic sports. On either side were arranged wide divans, covered with red drapery and high pillows. Small

stands were arranged in front of them. Various
parties were seated with novel inventions before
them, suggested by the minds of ingenious Turks, to
accomplish the destruction of the tobacco crop. The
members of the Elephant Club placed themselves on
the divans, and after they had arranged themselves to their satisfaction, their oriental friend
approached them, and gave to each a "programme"
of Turkish delicacies. Mr. Spout inquired what a
nargillê was, and was informed that it was a water-
pipe. Mr. Spout insisted that he preferred a pipe
wherein fire, rather than water, was the element
used. Mr. Boggs said he would take a *chibouk* on
trial. Mr. Spout coincided, and called also for a
chibouk. But Van Dam ordered three *nargillês*, one
for himself, another for Dropper, and a third for
Quackenbush. The *chibouks* were produced, and
Boggs and Spout commenced smoking in earnest.

In the mean time, the *nargillês* were produced for
the other members of the club. Van Dam backed
down at their first appearance. The glass vase, having in it water below and fire above, looked suspi-
cious, and added to that was a mysterious length of
hose, which was wound about in all directions, com
mencing at the fire, and running around the vase,
about the table legs, over the chair, back through

the rounds, about his legs, around his body, and finally came up over his shoulder, and terminated in a mouth-piece. Mr. Van Dam's first sensations, after these preliminaries had been arranged, were that he was in imminent danger of his life, and acting upon this impulse, he obstinately refused to go the *nargillê*, remarking, that they might be harmless enough in the hands of the Turks, who knew how to use such fire-arms, but he thought prudence dictated that he should keep clear of such diabolical inventions.

Dropper and Quackenbush, however, had no fears, but their drafts on the fire, through the hose, were not honored with smoke. They exhausted the atmosphere in their mouths, but get a taste of smoke they could not, and, in despair, Mr. Quackenbush called in the proprietor for an explanation of the mysteries of fumigating *à la Turque.* In compliance with the request, the gentleman informed the amateur Turks that they must inhale the smoke. Dropper protested that he wouldn't make his lungs a stove-pipe to oblige anybody—even the sultan and his sultanas—and he accordingly dropped the hose, and ordered a *chibouk.* Quackenbush, however, made the effort, but a spasmodic coughing put an end to further attempts, and the result was that another *chibouk* was called for. Each member of the club began to feel himself sufficiently etherealized to aspire to a position in a Mahomedan heaven, where he could be surrounded by the spirits of numberless beautiful *houris,* when the attention of Mr. Spout was attracted to a young gentleman, seated on a divan, in the rear of the apartment.

He was smoking a ponderous *chibouk*, and the
cloudy volumes sent forth from his mouth hung about
his form, quite obscuring him from sight. Occasionally, however, he would stop to breathe, which
gave the members of the club an opportunity to survey his appearance. He was a young man of about
twenty-two years, small in stature, with a pale, delicate skin, and light hair, plastered down by the barber's skill with exactness. He had no signs of beard
or moustache. He was evidently making mighty
efforts to become a Turk. He sat on the divan, with

his legs drawn up under him, adopting the Turkish mode of inhaling the smoke, and he followed one inhalation by another with such fearful rapidity that the first impulse of the uninitiated would have been to cry out fire.   But he evidently didn't sit easy, for after a few minutes, he pulled his legs out from under him and stretched them out at full length, to get out the wrinkles.   The Turkish manner of sitting was, evidently, attended with physical inconveniences, for, after about a dozen experimental efforts, he gave it up, put his heels on the table, and laid himself back against the cushions.   Still, however, he continued to smoke unremittingly (as if to make up in that what he lacked in ability to sit in the Turkish posture).   But it was soon manifest that the young man was suffering.   His face was deathly pale, and, dropping his *chibouk*, he called out for his oriental host.   The gentleman in the red cap appeared, and the sufferer informed him that he "felt so bad," and he placed his hand on his stomach, denoting that as the particular seat of his difficulty.   The benevolent Turk suggested exercise out of doors, and, as the elephant hunters were about going out, they offered to accompany him to his home.   The offer was accepted, and the youth, sick in the cause of Turkey, left, supported by Dropper and Quackenbush.

A walk of a few squares relieved the young gentleman of the extremely unpleasant sensations, when he begged leave to express his thanks to the gentlemen for their kindness. He took occasion to inform them that his name was John I. Cake, late a resident of an interior town in Illinois, where his parents now reside. He was, at present, living in New York with an uncle, who was a banker in Wall-street, under whose tuition he was learning rapidly how to make inroads upon the plunder of his neighbors, without being in danger of finding his efforts rewarded with board and lodging at the expense of State. He had been educated at a country college, and knew nothing of city life, except what he had seen in Wall street.

Mr. Spout said that he was very happy to have met him, and inquired whether he would like to have an opportunity of seeing the elephant.

Mr. John I. Cake said that nothing would please him better. Mr. Spout proceeded at once to inform him that the gentlemen who were present were members of an organization gotten up for that express purpose, and which was known among themselves as the Elephant Club; further he said to Mr. Cake, that if he desired to join, they would admi-

nister the obligation to him that evening, and initiate
him into the order.

Mr. Cake said by all means. At this time the
party had reached the front of a church, in the shadow of which they stopped. Mr. Spout, as Higholdboy, announced that the Elephant Club was now
organized. "Mr. Cake," said he, "step forward and
receive the obligation."

Mr. Cake did step forward with a bold and
determined step.

Mr. Spout continued : "Let your arm," said he,
"hang in an easy position from the right shoulder.
Now let the digits of your other hand point 'over
the left.' Now then, Mr. John I. Cake, late of the
State of Illinois, but now encircled with, the moral
atmosphere of Wall street, you do solemnly swear,
by the sacred horn spoons, that you desire to become a
member of the Elephant Club, that you are willing, on
becoming a member, to do as you please, unless it
pleases you to do something else ; that you will never
kick a big Irishman's dog, unless you think you are
smart enough to thrash his master ; that you will be
just as honest as you think the times will economi-
cally allow; that you will, under no circumstances
buy and smoke a 'penny grab,' so long as you have
philanthropic friends who will give you Havanas.

All of this you solemnly swear, so help you John Rogers."

"Perhaps," was the response of Mr. John I. Cake.

"Having given the correct response," said the Higholdboy, "you are pronounced a member of the Elephant Club, when you shall have duly favored us with the initiative sit down."

"Good!" said Mr. Cake, "where shall it be?"

"Wherever good oysters are to be procured," said Mr. Dropper.

"Here you are, then," remarked Quackenbush, as he pointed to a sign over a subterranean door-way, over which was inscribed the words,

"Here are the spot
Where good oysters is got."

The club descended into the saloon, and Mr. Cake called for six half dozens on the half shell.

Now, be it known to the readers of these records, that Mr. Cake was unacquainted with the perfection to which many departments of manual labor had reached, and being naturally of an inquiring turn of mind, he stayed outside to watch the feats of the young man who brandished the oyster-knife. This gentleman was an adept at his profession. With the most perfect grace of motion, he would lift the

4

oyster in his left hand, lay its edge gently on a small
iron standard, give that edge two delicate raps with
the butt of the oyster-knife as a signal to the oyster
that its turn had now come, when immediately the
shells would open, the upper half would jump off
and fall below, and the oyster would smile at the
young man as he took the knife, and delicately
stroked down its beard.   All of this transpired in a
very short period of time, which, with the artistic
grace displayed by the professor, was sufficient to

astound Mr. Cake.   Indeed, he had entirely forgotten his companions in his admiration of conchological anatomy.

The oysters were placed before the gentlemen, and partaken of with a relish.   But Mr. Cake had not seen enough to gratify his wishes.   He ordered another dose all around, and again took his position outside to watch the operation of divesting the oysters of one half of their natural exterior protection.   Without doubt, the young man's merits, at his particular vocation, were great; but Mr. Cake magnified them, in his intense admiration, most alarmingly.   To him, it seemed as if each particular oyster was waiting for its turn to come, and only wanted a wink from the young man, when it would jump into his grasp, proud that it was permitted so soon to be sacrificed by such a hand.   Mr. Cake was transfixed; he never moved his eyes until the second, third and fourth installment of shell-fish were served up.

Mr. Boggs then spoke about drinks.   Jonny protested that he never drank anything that would intoxicate — in fact, he was an uncompromising teetotaller.   Still, however, he had no objections to treating the crowd, as that would give him an opportunity to remain a few minutes more with the

object of his admiration. He continued to' watch
the motions, whilst his friends were doing justice to
the spirituous decoctions. At last Mr. Spout told
Jonny that it was time to go. Jonny went to the
bar, paid the bill, and, as the party regained the
street, Jonny Cake said, with a sigh, that he only
wished he were an oyster, that he, too, might be
the willing victim of that young man's knife. But,
inasmuch as he was not, it was his intention to gratify his desire to see the young man's manipulations
by coming every night until he was satisfied.

It is a fact which may be asserted, that Mr.
Jonny Cake, as the members of the club had now
learned to call him, with forty "oysters and the
fixens" on board, did not walk with much apparent
comfort.

The club stopped to deliberate, but in the midst
of their deliberations the City Hall bell sounded,
and instantly commenced all that furious uproar
peculiar to Gotham at the sound of an alarm of fire.
A crowd of screaming men and boys came tearing
along, dragging Engine No. 32½, which hung back
and jumped about, as if determined not to go at any
hazard. About half a block in advance of this crazy
throng rushed a frantic man, with a red shirt and a
tin trumpet. Each individual yelled as if the gene-

ral resurrection were at hand, and he under special obligations to wake up some particular friend.
The rheumatic engine held back with all its power,
and seemed, for the moment, endowed with a kind
of obstinate vitality. Now it threw its wheel round
a lamp-post, then it tumbled against the curb-stone,
then it ran its tongue into an awning, then affection-
ately embraced with its projecting arms a crockery-
wagon, and finally, with a kind of inanimate dogged
determination not to go ahead, in turning a short
corner, it leaped triumphantly astride a hydrant,
where it stuck. The men tugged, but the engine
held fast; the frantic man in the red shirt came
tearing back; he had gone far enough ahead to see
that 13¼'s boys had got their stream on the fire, and
he was furious at the delay. One mighty jerk, and
the men and boys were piled in a huge kicking mass
on the pavement, which phenomenon was occasioned
by the unexpected breaking of the rope. The rope
was tied, and by a united effort directed at the
wheels, the brakes, the tongue, and every get-at-able
point, the machine was again started, protesting, with
creaks, and groans, and various portentous rum-
blings in its inner works, against the roughness of
its treatment.

The frantic red-shirt-man howled through his

trumpet that Hose 24⅜ was coming. The boys looked back, and Hose 24⅜ *was* coming. Hose 24⅜ came alongside. Hose 24⅜ tried to go by. Hose 24⅜ was evidently striving to get to the fire in advance of her betters, but Hose 24⅜ couldn't do it— for, at this interesting juncture, 32½'s fellows waked up to their work, and the race began. Single gentlemen got into doorways, or crawled under carts; the ladies who were in the street at that time of night disappeared down oyster-cellars; the M. P.s probably went through the coal-holes, for not one was at that instant " visible to the naked eye." Stages, to get out of the way, turned down alleys so narrow that they had to be drawn out backwards; an express-wagon was run into, and wrecked on a pile of bricks; an early milk-cart was left high and dry on a mountain of oyster-shells; a belated hand-cart-man deserted his vehicle in the middle of the street, and it was instantly demolished, while the owner was only preserved from a similar fate by being knocked gently over a picket-fence into an area, where there couldn't anybody get at him. In the height and very fury of the race, the crowd rushed upon the Elephantines, who were gazing in fancied security at the mixed-up spectacle before them. In an instant they were all inextricably

entangled in the rush; those that escaped 32½ were
caught up instantly by 24⅜, and those who got away
from 24⅜, were seized upon by 32½. It was no use
resisting—on they must go. The ponderosity of
John Spout was no protection to him; nor did the
lankness of Dusenbury Quackenbush, and the unre-
liable appearance of his legs, avail him anything.
The quiet inoffensiveness of Van Dam was not
respected; no regard was paid to the philosophical
composure of Mr. Remington Dropper. The youthful
face of Jonny Cake, too, availed nothing in his favor.
Mr. Boggs became involved, and all were irretrieva-
bly mingled with the howling demi-devils who were
racing for the miniature purgatory, the flames from
which could now be plainly seen. It was "No. 1,
round the corner," the residence of "My Uncle,"
and each one was anxious to redeem his individual
effects without going through the formality of pay-
ing charges and giving up the tickets.

But their very anxiety was a serious bar to their
rapid progress : and the two machines were jammed
together by the zealous rivals. Hard words ensued,
and a general row was the instant and legitimate
result. Quackenbush was complimented with a lick
over the head with a trumpet, in the hands of the
frantic red-shirt-man, who accused him of locking the

tongue of 24⅝ into 32½'s wheel. Dropper had his hat knocked over his eyes, and thereupon, his indignation being roused, he hit out, right and left. His first vigorous blow inflicted terrific damage upon the amiable countenance of his best friend, Mr. Van Dam, and the very first kick he gave upset Mr. John Spout

upon the protruding stomach of a man who had been knocked down with a spanner. John quickly recovered himself, and hit Van Dam a clip in the sinister optic, which placed that useful member in a state of temporary total eclipse. The battle became general, and each man waged an indiscriminate war upon his neighbor. Between the affectionate thrashing they gave each other, and the indiscriminate kicks and punches they received from outsiders, the Elephantines were well pommelled. By the time 32½ and

24§ had got out of the muss, and were fairly on their way to the fire again, Mr. John Spout was the only one of that fraternal band visible on his feet. Dropper was doubled up across a hydrant, Van Dam was comfortably reposing on his back, in the middle of the street, while Quackenbush was sitting on him, trying to wipe the blood out of his eyes, and to ascertain, as nearly as possible, the number of teeth he had swallowed. But when the members came together to make mutual explanations, Jonny Cake was *non est.* Great, indeed, was the cry that was heard after the missing member. Quackenbush bellowed out, in a heavy, sonorous voice, that the difficulty was all past, when Jonny's shrill voice was heard in response. The voice proceeded from an empty molasses hogshead, into which Jonny had jumped, during the melee, for safety. His brother-members released him from his situation, and, when he was once more on Gotham's pavement, he was literally a sweet case. Dirty sugar adhered to every part of his exterior. Explanations were then made, and the members proceeded to shake hands all round, except Mr. Dropper, who couldn't shake hands with anybody, because some one had upset a bucket of tar on his fingers, and he couldn't get it off.

The matter being at length arranged to the satis-

4*

faction of all concerned, they adjourned from the
sidewalk to a beer-shop, where they washed their
faces, pinned up the rents in their pantaloons, and
got the jams out of their hats, as well as they could
upon so short a notice. They then found their way
to the club-room, held a council, and without a great
deal of deliberation, it was resolved, every man for
himself:

That, to prevent the future possibility of all the
members of the club having black eyes at the same
time, the members would, from this time forth, pursue their investigations singly, or in pairs—the optical adornment of a single person being bearable, but
for all the club to be simultaneously thus affected,
was a phenomenon not down in the bills.

The club then adjourned for convalescence.

First Evening with the Club.

"Dogs bark."—SHAKSPEARE.

As soon as the members of the Elephant Club had recovered their normal appearance, each issued forth alone to catch further glimpses of the colossal quadruped of the metropolis. Each was assiduous in pursuing his investigations, and all manifested a spirit of self-denial worthy of martyrs in the cause of scientific research. The quantity of bad liquors they drank in forming new acquaintances, it were useless to estimate; the horrible cigars they smoked with those acquaintances are beyond computation, and yet they never flagged for a moment. After a few days, thus passed, the Higholdboy thought it time the club should hear the reports of its members. He, accordingly, put up on the bulletin a notice, stating that he expected the attendance of every member on a certain evening.

The evening came, and with it came the members.

The weather was sufficiently warm to admit of the windows being up, and a fine, cooling draught of air passed through the apartment. The gentlemen filled their pipes and proceeded to take it easy. Mr. Dropper hung himself upon two chairs; Boggs stretched himself upon a sofa; Van Dam took off his coat, rolled it up for a pillow, and laid himself out on the floor. Quackenbush put an easy-chair by the door, and seated himself there to act as sentinel. Mr. Spout, the Higholdboy, moved his official chair up to one of the windows, turned the back upon his fellow-members, seated himself, raised his feet to the window-casing, and said that, with his eyes looking out between the toes of his boots upon the tiles and chimney-pots, it could not be said he had seen any disorderly conduct, if the members should see fit to vary the monotony of the proceedings by getting up an extemporized row among themselves. Jonny Cake alone seemed aware that a necessity existed for the exhibition of proper dignity on the part of the meeting. He sat by the table proudly erect. His standing collar, neatly-tied cravat, and scrupulously clean exterior, corresponded with his prim deportment.

It became a serious question who should open his budget of experience first. There was no rule to coerce a member to commence; consequently, appeals were made to the magnanimity of each other. These were irresistible, and all suddenly became willing and even anxious to make the beginning.

Mr. Dropper, however, got the floor first. He insisted that he was not in the habit of appearing in large assemblies as a prominent participant in the proceedings, and, in consideration of this fact, he ventured to hope that his incipient efforts would not be judged of harshly.

Mr. Dropper's spasmodic modesty excited the boisterous mirth of his fellow-members.

Mr. Remington Dropper commenced:

"Gentlemen of the Elephant Club," said he, "the subject which I have to present for your consideration this evening is a remarkable instance of the *genus homo* which I accidentally came across in my peregrinations a few evenings since. I was returning home from the theatre, and in passing a door-way in Broadway, I discovered a man seated on the stone step, with his form reclining against the door-casing. The gas-light shone directly in his face, which revealed to me the fact that he was asleep. The singularity of his personal appearance could not fail to attract my attention, and I stopped to study his form, features, and dress, to determine, if I could, who and what he was. His face had evidently been put up askew. The corner of his mouth, the eye and eyebrow on one side were inclined downward, giving him a demure and melancholy look; but on the other side they were inclined upwards, which made that side show a continued grin. A front view of his face was suggestive of both joy and melancholy, which was equal to no expression at all, as the expression on one side offset that of the other. His coat, which was buttoned tightly about him, was neither a dress nor a frock, but the skirts were rounded off in front, making it a compromise between the two. His pants were also a go-between; they were neither white nor black, but in point of color, were a pepper-and-salt formation. The leg on one side was rolled up. On one foot was a boot, on the other a shoe. He wore a very dirty collar, which, on the laughing side of his face was Byronic, and on the solemn side, uncompromisingly erect. His hat was an antiquated shanghae—black on the crown and light underneath the brim. If a noun, he was certainly a very uncommon, but not strictly a proper noun. If a verb, he seemed to be passive. The tense of his general appearance it would be difficult to determine. Strictly, it was neither past nor present, nor was it in accordance with my ideas of the future. To a certain extent it was all three. His seedy exterior was the remains of the past, existing in the present, and existing prospectively in the future. His mood was subjunctive, full of doubt and uncertainty. Judging from his entire appearance, I could come to no other conclusion as respects his character, than that he was a combination of ups and downs, a concentration of small differences, a specimen of non-committalism in everything except an entire abstinence from water used as a means of purifying his body externally, and his clothing. His red nose led me to suspect that he did not bathe with cold water to an alarming extent inwardly. The individual was remarkable, not for what he was, but for what he was not.

"Such were my thoughts, gentlemen, and I determined to awake the unconscious sleeper, to see how far my conclusions were right. I shook him well, and accompanied my act with a peremptory order to 'get up.' After a moment he roused himself and looked at me, but immediately dropped his eyes. I commenced a dialogue with him, which, as near as I can recollect, was as follows:

" 'What are you doing here?' said I.

" 'Dun'no,' was the response.

" 'You're certainly quite drunk.'

" 'Likely.'

" ' That is an offence against the law.'

" ' Des'say.'

" ' You've been arrested for drunkenness before.'

" ' Werry like.   But I 'aven't been a doin' nuthin' helse.'

" ' But I've arrested you before,' said I, playing the policeman, in order to continue the conversation.

" ' Des'say, hofficer; but did I hoffer any resistance ?'

" ' Your weight did.'

" ' Vas it wiolent ?'

" ' You were too drunk to make any violent resistance.'

" ' Des'say; I honly inquired for hinformation.'

" ' What's your name ?'

" ' Vich name do you vant to know ?'

" ' Your whole name, of course.'

" ' Bobinger Thomas.'

" ' Where were you born, Thomas ?'

" ' Hingland.'

" ' What is your business ?'

" ' My perwession ?'

" ' Yes.'

" ' It's warious.   I never dabbled with law, physic, or diwinity.'

" ' I asked you what your profession is—not what it isn't.'

" ' My perwession now, or vot it used to vos ?'

" ' Your present profession, of course.'

" ' Vell—nuthin'.'

" ' Well, what was your profession in the past ?'

" ' Vot do you vant to know for ?'

" ' I shall answer no questions; but you must. Now tell me what your past profession was.'

" ' Dogs.'

" ' Are you a dog-fancier ?'

" ' Poss'bly ; I fancies dogs.'

" ' What breed of dogs do you fancy ?'

" 'Them as I gets in Jersey.'

" 'What do you do with the dogs that you get there ?'

" ' I vouldn't go into the business if I vos in your sitivation. It don't pay any more, 'cause there's so many coves as has inwested. I left 'cause it vos hoverdid.'

" ' I hadn't the slightest intention of going into the business. I asked you for information.'

" 'Glad to 'ear you say so. I vos halmost hutterly ruined in it.'

" ' Well, what do you do with the dogs ?'

" ' I doesn't follow the perwession no more.'

" ' I asked you what you did with the dogs you picked up in New Jersey.'

" 'They muzzles dogs now more than they did vonce.'

" 'Tell me what you did with the dogs.'

" ' If you nab a cove for gettin' drunk vot do they do vith 'im ?'

" ' Are you going to answer my question ?'

" 'Vill they let me off if I tell vere I got the liquor ?'

" ' Look here, Thomas, answer my question.'

" ' Vot do they do vith the coves as sells ?'

" 'I shan't trifle with you any longer. If you don't tell me what you do with the dogs, I shall enter a charge of vagrancy against you.'

" 'Vell, I didn't sell 'em for sassengers.'

" 'What did you sell them for ?'

" 'I didn't sell 'em.'

" 'How did you dispose of them ?'

" 'Is old Keene varden of the penitentiary now ?'

" 'Tell me, now, what you did with the dogs.'

" 'I took 'em to the dog pound.'

" 'What did you do with them there ?'

" 'Vy, doesn't they muzzle cats the same as dogs ?'

" 'Look here, Thomas, you must answer my question without equivocation. I want to understand the details of this dog-business. What did you do with them at the dog-pound ?'

" 'For hevery dog as ve takes to the pound ve gets an 'arf a slum.'

" 'Then it seems you caught your dogs in New Jersey, brought them to the New York dog-pound, and claimed for your philanthropic exertions the reward of a half a dollar, offered by ordinance for every dog caught within the limits of New York ?'

" 'Vell, if you'd been born into the perwession, you couldn't have understood its vays better.'

" ' You are a sweet subject, certainly.'

" ' Des'say.'

" ' Are you not ashamed of yourself, to be found lying drunk in door-ways?'

" ' B'lieve so.'

" ' Are you not certain you are?'

" ' Prob'bly.'

" ' Did you drink liquor to-night?'

" ' P'r'aps.'

" ' Where did you get it?'

" ' Dun'no.'

" ' What kind was it?'

" ' I halvays 'ad a passion for gin.'

" ' Was it gin you drank to-night?'

" ' Des'say.'

" ' Are you not sure that it was?'

" ' Mebbee.'

" ' How often do you drink?"

" ' Honly ven I've got the blunt to pay. Dutchmen vont trust now.'

" ' Did you have any money to-night?'

" ' Likely.'

" ' How did you get it?'

" ' 'Oldin' an 'orse for a cove.'

" ' How much did you get for that?'

" ' A shillin.'

"' With that you bought gin ?'

" ' Prob'bly.'

" ' And got drunk ?'

" ' Poss'bly.'

" ' Thomas, where do you live ?'

" ' Noveres, in p'tickler.'

" ' Where do you eat ?'

" ' Vere the wittles is.'

" ' Where do you sleep ?'

" ' Anyveres, so that the M. P.s can't nab me.'

" ' You ought to be sent to Blackwell's Island as a vagrant.'

" ' Des'say.'

" ' You've been there, have you not ?'

" ' Mebbee.'

" ' Don't you know whether you've been there or not ?'

" ' P'r'aps.'

" ' Are you certain of anything ?'

" ' Dun'no.'

" ' Now, Thomas,' said I, in conclusion, ' I am going to let you off this time, but I hope you will keep sober in the future. Now, here is a quarter for you, to pay for your lodging to-night.'

"Thomas, the non-committalist, accepted the silver

"I concluded to ask him one more question, in hopes to get a direct and positive answer.

"'Will you use that money to pay for a bed?' I asked.

"'Des'say,' said he, upon which I vamosed."

The Higholdboy raised himself from his official seat before the window, turned round, got on his knees in the chair, leaned his head on his hands and his arms on the chair-back, and whilst everybody was still and quiet, he called out, in a stentorian voice, "Order." The effect of this peremptory demand was to induce considerable disorder, as no one was willing to be regarded out of order, even by implication, without some foundation. Everybody talked and nobody listened, except Mr. Dropper, and it was not until Mr. Quackenbush had stuffed a ham sandwich down the throat of the Higholdboy, thrown a box of sardines at the head of Van Dam, tipped over the timid Boggs, and poured a lemonade down the throat of Jonny Cake, that they would consent to hear what he desired to say.

"Gentlemen," said Quackenbush, "that's a remarkably fine story, isn't it?"

"Des'say," said Spout.

"Werry like," responded Van Dam.

"Mebbee," replied Jonny Cake.

"Likely," remarked Boggs, as he picked himself up, preparatory to letting himself down in three chairs.

Mr. Spout left his chair, and moved to that particular locality in the apartment where the bell-pull, leading to the bar below, was situated. He gave sundry pulls in accordance with the previously-arranged system of telegraphing, and in a few minutes they were answered by a young gentleman, with a tin waiter in his hands, on which were placed divers decoctions, which stand in better repute outside of total abstinence societies than inside. Each took his mixture until it came to Jonny Cake, when the Higholdboy passed over to him a mild beverage, called a port wine sangaree. Johnny refused to accept it, and announced that he was strict in his adherence to principle—that he never indulged in anything which could intoxicate. A lemonade he would indulge in sometimes, but a port wine sangaree—never—*never*—NEVER.

When Jonny Cake had finished his indignant repudiation of the port wine sangaree amid the cheering of his fellow members, Mr. James George Boggs arose. He mounted a chair, and made an effort to speak. He was greeted with loud applause.

As soon as these manifestations had subsided, he said :

"Fellow-citizens (applause); I may say that it is with feelings of the most profound gratification (loud applause), that I meet, this evening, the members of the illustrious Elephant Club (continued applause), of which I am an unpretending and obscure member (renewed applause). Gentlemen, I do not like to appear as an apologist, and much less an apologist for my own shortcomings (loud and continued applause). Gentlemen, I protest against your unwarranted interference when I am trying to be funny (applause and cheers). I am a modest man, and I am unwilling to stand here to be fooled with (enthusiastic applause); Mr. Dropper, if you don't shut up your mouth, I'll knock your moustache down your throat (tremendous applause). Mr. Spout, you are the Higholdboy of this club, but I'll hit you with a brick if you don't keep better order. (Cries of " Order !" " Order !") If you'll stop your blasted noise, there will be no trouble about order. (Cries of "Go on !") Well, gentlemen, as I was saying that—that—that—where the devil did I leave off? (Applause and laughter.) There, you see that you have broken the thread of my remarks. (Cries of " Good !") Yes, it may be fun for you, but, as the boy said to the frogs, it's death to me (laughter).   No, I mean as the Death said to the boys, it's frogs to—(renewed laughter).   Go to thunder!   I am not going to make speeches to such a set a young rascals as you are."   (More applause.)

As soon as order had restored itself, the Highold-boy ordered, at his own expense, a glass of apple-jack for Mr. Boggs, with the view of expressing, through it, his full and thorough appreciation of Boggs's oratory.   Mr. Boggs accepted it.   Inquiry was then made of Mr. Boggs as to what he had desired to say in his speech.   He stated substantially, that, having been engaged in loafing about, and doing nothing, he had had no time to prepare a contribution for the entertainment of the club.

So completely had the eloquence of Mr. Boggs riveted the attention of the club, that they had hardly made a commencement in disposing of the beverages which had been ordered; Mr. Dropper proposed that, as Johnny Cake was not to be employed in drinking, he having ignored the proffered port wine sangaree, he should occupy their time by relating his experience.   To this he expressed his willingness to accede.   He stated, however, that he had been on a flying visit to Illinois since his initiation into the Elephantine order, and that he was consequently unable to furnish them with any experience of an interesting nature, in New York. But some interesting incidents had occurred on a railroad train, which he had undertaken to note down, with the view of reading to the club.

Mr. Johnny Cake here produced a roll of manuscripts, which, after he had straightened up his collar, he proceeded to read. The manuscript read as follows:—

"I do not propose, now, to give you a glimpse of anything within the city. In fact, it is my intention to inflict upon you an extra-metropolitan scene, which I recently witnessed, and which, though funny, was not comfortable, and I don't care about experiencing it again.

The section of country to which your attention is called was flat—positively flat—comparatively stale, and superlatively unprofitable. It was a western prairie marsh, the home of gigantic frogs, the abiding place of water-snakes and musk-rats; where flourished in luxuriant profusion, bulrushes, water-cresses, pond-lilies, and such like amphibious and un-get-at-able vegetables. Through that particular locality a train of cars was not only seen, but heard going at 2'40" speed over a pile-bridge, made across a Michigan swamp, by driving black-oak logs endwise into the mud. The people therein were covered with dust, as thickly as if each man had been

a locomoting Pompeii, each woman a perambulating
Herculaneum, and some vagrant Vesuvius had been
showering ashes on them all for a month. They
were lying about loose in the cars, after the ordinary
fashion of people on a tedious railway journey;
curled up in some such ungraceful and uneasy posi-
tions as the tired beasts of a strolling menagerie
probably assume in their cages during their forced
marches across the country. To carry out the
parallel, the conductor came along at irregular intervals, and with deliberate and premeditated malignity,
stirred up the passengers, as if they were actually
animals on exhibition, and he really was their
keeper, and wanted to make them growl. And this
conductor, in common with conductors in general,
deserves notice for the diabolical ingenuity which he
displayed in forcing from his helpless victims the
greatest number of growls in a limited space of time.

The cars had just left the flourishing prairie city of
Scraggville, which contains seven houses and a
tavern, and a ten-acre lot for a church, in the centre
of which the minister holds forth now from a cedar
stump. At the tavern, dinner had been served up,
and the conductor, according to the usual custom, had
started the train as soon, without waiting for his passengers to eat anything, as the money was collected.

The population of our train, which exceeded that of the great city of Scraggville by about one hundred and seventy persons, had composed itself for a short nap, and the various individuals had settled as nearly into their old places as possible, when a man, remarkable for a particularly lofty shirt-collar, a wooden leg, and an unusual quantity of dust on the bridge of his nose, began to sing. He commenced that touching ballad, now so popular, " the affecting history of Vilikins and his Dinah." The pathos of his words, added to the unusual power of his voice, waked up his right-hand neighbor, before he had proceeded any further than to inform the listeners that,

" Vilikins vas a-valking " ——

This neighbor who was so suddenly aroused, and who was distinguished by a steeple-crowned hat, did not appear to care *where* Vilikins was a-walking, or to take much interest in the particulars of the said walk, for he immediately turned on the other side, tied himself up in a worse knot than he was in before, and attempted to sleep again. He had in so doing shaken from the top of his mountainous hat about half a peck of cinders, directly into the mouth of the vocalist. The latter gentleman, however, seemed nothing disconcerted by this unexpected pulverulent donation, but, removing those particles which most interfered with his vocal apparatus, he proceeded with his melody.   This time he progressed as far as to state emphatically that,

"Vilikins vas a-valkin' in his garding one day,"

And was about to add the explanatory notes, that it was the "back garding," when his left-hand neighbor emerged from a condition of somnolency into a state of unusual wakefulness.

The most noticeable thing about this last named individual was the optical fact that he had but one eye.   And as this solitary orb was partially filled with the dust which had accumulated therein, during a ten hours' nap in a rail-car, over a sandy road, with a headwind, it might be supposed that his facilities for visual observation were somewhat abridged. This did not prove, however, to be the case, for with a single glance of this encumbered optic, he seemed to take in the character of the singer, and to make up his mind instanter that he was a good fellow and a man to be acquainted with.

Acting promptly upon this extemporaneous opinion, he held out his hand with the remark:

"I don't want to interfere with any arrangements you have made, stranger, but here's my hand, and my name's Wagstaff—let's be jolly."

The singer had by this time got to the chorus of his song, and although he took the extended hand, his only immediate reply to the observations of one-eyed Wagstaff, was "too ral li, too ral li, too ral li la," which he repeated with an extra shake on the last "la," before he condescended to answer. And even then his observation, though poetic, was not particularly coherent or relevant. It was couched in the following language.

"Jolly? yes, we'll be jolly. Old King Cole was a jolly old soul, and a jolly old soul was he. He called for his pipe and he called for his bowl— wonder if he got it? My name is Dennis, my mother's maiden name was Moore, so that if I'd been born before she married, I'd have been a poet, which I'm sorry to say, don't think it, for I ain't. I'm glad to see you, Mr. Wagstaff, and as you say *you're* jolly, and propose that we shall *all* be jolly, perhaps you'll favor me by coming out strong on the second and fourth lines of this chorus.

"I'll do my little utmost," said Wagstaff.

And he *did* do his little utmost with a will, and their united voices croaked up again the first man

with the steeple-crowned hat, who hadn't got his eyes fairly opened before *he* joined in the chorus too, and he gave his particular attention to it, and put in so many unexpected cadenzas and quavers which the composer never intended, and shakes that nobody else *could* put in, and trills that his companions couldn't keep up with, that he fairly astonished his hearers. And he didn't stop when they did, but kept singing "tooral li tooral," with unprecedented variations, and wouldn't hold up for Dennis to sing the verses, and wouldn't wait for Wagstaff to take breath; but kept right on, now putting a long shake on "tooral," now an unheard of trill on "looral,"

now coming out with redoubled force on the final
" la," and then starting off again, as if his voice had
run away with him and he didn't want to stop it, but
was going to sing a perpetual chorus of unceasing
" toorals " and never ending " loorals."

For fifteen minutes his harmony was allowed
uninterrupted progress, but at length Wagstaff,
putting his hand over his mouth, thereby smother-
ing, in its infancy, a strain of extraordinary power,
addressed him thus :

" I don't want to interfere with any of your little
arrangements, stranger, but, if you don't stop that
noise, I'll knock your head off. What do you mean
by intruding your music upon other people's music,
and thus mixing the breed? Don't you try to swal-
low my fist, you can't digest it."

The latter part of this address was called forth by
the frantic efforts of the unknown amateur to get his
mouth away from behind Wagstaff's hand, which
he at length accomplished, and when he had
recovered his breath he made an effort to speak.
The musical fiend, however, had got too strong possession of him to give up on so short a notice, and
he was unable to speak more than ten words without
introducing another touch of the magical chorus.
The address with which he first favored his compa-

nions ran something after the following fashion and sounded as if he might have been the identical Vilikins, unexpectedly recovered from the effects of the " cup of cold pison," or prematurely resurrected from the "same grave," wherein he had been disposed by the " cruel parient " by the side of the lamented " Dinah."

" My friends, don't interrupt the concert—too ral li, too ral li, too ral li la. I'll explain presently —with a too ral li, too ral li, too ral li la. I'm delighted to meet you—allow me to introduce myself—ral li la—I am a professional—loo ral li, loo ral li—man—ral li la—my name is Moses Overdale—with my loo ral li, loo ral li, loo ral li la."

Here he stopped, evidently by a violent exertion, and shook hands with each of the others, and afforded such a view of his personal appearance as satisfied the individual of the solitary optic, and his companion of the vegetable leg, that they had fallen in with another original—added to the fact, with which they were already well acquainted, that he had a powerful, though not very controllable voice. Other things about the newly-discovered person showed him to be a man far above, or below, or, at least, differing from, the common run of people one meets in a railroad-car. His face, had it

5*

been visible to the naked eye, through the surrounding thicket of hair, might have passed for good-looking; but the hirsute crop which flourished about his head was something really remarkable. If each hair had possessed as many roots as a scrub oak sapling, and had grown the wrong way, with the roots out, there couldn't have been more ; or if each individual hair had been grafted with a score of thrifty shoots, and each of them, in turn, had given off a multitude of sandy-colored sprouts, and each separate sprout had taken an unconquerable aversion to every other sprout, and was striving to grow in an independent direction of its own, there wouldn't have been a more abundant display of hair, growing towards a greater variety of hitherto unknown points of compass. It was so long that it concealed his neck and shoulders, and you could only suppose he had a throat from the certainty that he had a mouth. And even the mouth was in its turn ornamented with an overhanging moustache, of a subdued rat-color, which also was long, running down the corners of the jaw, and joining the rest of the beard on the neck below. A shirt-collar, turned down over his coat, was dimly visible whenever the wind was strong enough to lift the superincumbent hair.

Taking into account the physical curtailments of Overdale's companions, the trio consisted of about two men and a half.

Dennis now proposed that they should go on with the song, he volunteering to sing the verses, and requesting the reinforcements to show their strength when he said, " *Chorius* "—the mention of music excited Overdale's harmonic devil again, and he was obliged to twist his neckerchief until he was black in the face, to choke down an embryo, " too-ral," which ran to his lips before the cue came, and seemed to insist upon an immediate and stormy exit ; by dint of the most suffocating exertions he succeeded in keeping back the musical torrent until the end of the verse, when it broke forth with a vengeance.

And then Wagstaff struck in, and Dennis took a long breath, and *he* struck in ; and they waked up a couple of children, and *they* struck in ; and Dennis put his wooden leg on the tail of a dog, and *he* struck in ; and the locomotive put on the final touch, by shrieking with a frightful yell, as if it had boiled down into one, the squalls of eleven hundred freshly-spanked babies.

And they kept on, Dennis singing, in a masterly manner, the historical part ; the charms of Dinah

the barbarity of the cruel parient, the despair of
Vilikins, the death and burial of the unfortunate
"lovyers," their subsequent ghastly reappearance to
the cruel parient, and his final remorse, had all been
related; the "chorus of tender maidens" had been
pathetically sung by the musical trio; the "chorus
of cruel and unnatural parients," had been indignantly disposed of; the "chorus of pisoned young"
women," had been spasmodically executed: the
"chorus of agonized young men, with an awful pain
in the stummack," had been convulsively performed;
the "chorus of cold corpuses," had been sepulchrally
consummated; and the musical enthusiasts were laying
out their most lugubrious strength on the "concluding dismal chorus of gloomy apparitions," when the
concert was interrupted by the train running off the
track and pitching a part of the passengers into a
sand-bank on the right, throwing the remainder into
frog-pond on the left, and gently depositing the
engineer on a brush heap, where he was afterwards
discovered with the bell-rope in his hand, and his
legs covered up by the smoke-pipe.

It was soon ascertained that no very serious
damage was done, beyond the demolition of the
engine, which had left the rail without cause or pro-
vocation, and was now lying by the side of the road

with its head in the mud, wrong end to, bottom side up, roasting itself brown, steaming itself yellow, and smoking itself black, like an insane cooking-stove turned out-doors for misbehavior.

Overdale got out of the sand without assistance, and, save a black eye, and a peck or two of sand and gravel in his hair, was none the worse for the accident. Wagstaff crawled out of the frog pond, looking as dripping and juicy as a he-mermaid; while Dennis, though unconscious of any painful hurt, had sustained so serious a fracture of his wooden leg, that he found it necessary to splice it with an ironwood sapling before he could navigate.

It being discovered that the danger was over, and that there was nothing more to fear, the ladies, as in

duty bound, began to faint; one old lady fainted, and
fell near the engine; happening, however, to sit down
in a puddle of hot water, she got up quicker than
she went down; young lady, rather pretty, fainted
and fell into the arms of four or five gentlemen who
were waiting to receive her; another young lady
fainted, and didn't fall into anybody's arms, being
cross-eyed and having a wart on her nose; maiden
lady, ancient and fat, got near a good-looking man
with a big moustache, and giving notice of her
intention by a premonitory squall, shut her eyes, and
fell towards moustache; she had better, however,
have kept her eyes open, for moustache, seeing her
coming, and making a hasty estimate of her probable weight, stepped aside, and the gentle creature
landed in a clump of Canada thistles, whence she
speedily recovered herself, and looked fiery indignation at moustache, who bore it like a martyr; young
lady in pantalets and curls tried it, but, being inex-
perienced, and not having taken the precaution to
pick out a soft place to fall, in case there didn't anybody catch her, she bumped her head on a stone, and
got up with a black eye; jealous married lady, seeing her husband endeavoring to resuscitate a plump-
looking miss, immediately extemporized a faint herself, and fell directly across the young miss aforesaid.

contriving as she descended, to break her husband's
spectacles by a malicious dig with her elbow ; in fact
the ladies all fainted at least once apiece, and those
who received the most attention had an extra spasm or
two before their final recovery, while the vicious old
maids whom nobody cared for, invariably fell near
the best-looking girls, and went into furious convul-
sions, so that they could kick them in the tender
places without its being suspected that their intentions were not honorable.

During this characteristic female performance, our
musical trio had not been idle. Dennis had been
busily engaged in splicing his wooden leg. Wagstaff had seized a bucket from the disabled engine,
and nearly drowned three or four unfortunate
females with dirty water from the frog-pond. Overdale was attracted to the side of a blue-eyed girl,
who had swooned in a clean place, behind a conceal-
ing blackberry bush, and he had rubbed the skin off
her hands in his benevolent exertions to " bring her
to," and had meanwhile liberally peppered her face
and neck with gravel-stones and sand, from the stock
which had accumulated in his hair when he was first
pitched into the sand-bank.

Everybody was eventually convalescent, and

likely to recover from the damage which nobody
had sustained; the gentlemen had repented of the
prayers which they had not said, and were now
swearing ferociously about their fractured pocket-
companions, and their broken cigars; and the ladies
were regaling each other with multitudinous
accounts of miraculous escapes, from the horrible
accidents which might have killed everybody, but
hadn't hurt anybody. Another engine was sent for,
and the cars ran to the end of the railroad, seventy
miles, before the women stopped talking, or the men
got anything to drink.

The musical trio, whose united chorus had been
so suddenly interrupted, met at the bar of the
nearest tavern for the first time since the run off;
their greeting was peculiar, but characteristic; when
they came in sight of each other, they didn't speak
a word, until they solemnly joined hands and finished
the "too ral li la," which they hadn't had the leisure
to complete at the time of their sudden separation.
Overdale, true to his ruling passion, wouldn't stop
when the others did, but was going on with an extra
"tooral li, looral li," when Wagstaff presented a
glass of strong brandy and water at him; the plan
succeeded; he stopped in the midst of a most aston-

ishing shake on the first "looral," and merely remarking, "To be continued," he yielded, a passive captive to the fluid conqueror.

Subsequent conversations disclosed their future plans, and it was discovered that they were all journeying to the same place, New York city; and that their several visits had one common object, to see the mysteries of the town. An agreement, which I overheard, was quickly made, that they should remain together, and pursue, in company, their investigations.

They proceeded harmoniously on their journey, singing "Vilikins" between meals every day; and when Overdale couldn't stop in the chorus at the the proper time, Wagstaff corked him up with a corn-cob, which he carried in his pocket for that purpose.

It so happened that I continued on the same trains of cars with this interesting trio of eccentrici-ties, until we took the steamboat at the Dutch village, where the State Legislature meets. After the last verse of their customary evening hymn had been sung, with a strong chorus, as they were about to shelve themselves in their state-rooms for the night, I heard Overdale remark to his companions:

"When shall we three meet again? In thunder, lightning, or—well, no matter where. Dennis, you

see this black eye; I have to make this particular
request, that if this steamboat blows up in the night,
and you take a fancy to black anybody's eye, you'll
pick out somebody's else."

"I didn't black your eye; what do you mean?"

Overdale explained thus: "I could a tale unfold,
which would—but I won't—I'll tell you how
it happened, nothing extenuate or set down aught in
malice. When that locomotive ran off the track,
the shock threw us both, as you are aware, about
fifteen feet straight up in the air—as I was going up,
you were coming down, and you were practising
some kind of an original pigeon-wing with your
wooden leg, and, in one of its fantastic gyrations, it
came in contact with my visual apparatus, and
damaged my personal beauty to the extent you see;
—don't do it any more, that's all, my friend, don't
do it any more."

Dennis expressed himself exceedingly sorry—
"Overdale, my hairy friend," said he, "at the particular time you speak of, that leg was not under my
control, and I am not accountable for the misbehavior of that leg; but I solemnly promise that, if we
are blown up before morning, if I see which way
you go, I will do my best to travel in a different
direction."

Each of us, myself included, then went to his state-room, achieved his allotted shelf, rolled himself into so small a ball that the narrow blankets would cover him, and laid in feverish restlessness, awaiting that morning bell which should summon him to disperse himself into his pantaloons, go on deck, and catch the first glimpse of smoky Gotham, the home of the undiluted elephant."

"Hooror for Johnny," said Mr. Spout, as he rushed towards that individual to offer his congratulations. The other members followed suit, and Johnny, anticipating that he would be favored with a bear-like hug, more boisterous than pleasant, unless he acted promptly to prevent such a consummation, ran into one corner, squared off, and threatened to show an immoderate pugnacity, if they made any immoderate demonstrations of fraternal affection. The language and action of Johnny had the effect to check the enthusiasm of his friends, and they resumed their places. Johnny then came out, and made a peremptory demand of Mr. Spout that he telegraph to the saloon below for a lemonade for his (Johnny's) private consumption. Mr. Spout announced the impossibility of acceding to Johnny's demand, as there had been no signal agreed upon which should indicate to the individual below that a

lemonade was wanted. Johnny said that he could
not hold Mr. Spout to a strict accountability on that
occasion, but if he did not arrange a signal to indicate his future wants, he should proceed to expel
Mr. Spout from the club. Under existing circumstances, he should go down below and order person-
ally a strong lemonade, to be made of considerable
lemon, some sugar, and a good deal of water. Johnny
disappeared through the door. He had been gone
three minutes, by Quackenbush's bull's-eye silver
watch, which he says keeps excellent time as long as
he hires a boy to move the balance-wheel, when the
Higholdboy arose, and proposed "The health of the
Elephant—may his shadow never be less," which was
to be drunk in silence, standing. All the members
had assumed an erect position, required for the performance of this imposing ceremony, when a yell of
such prodigious dimensions, entitling it to be called
a roar, followed by a most extraordinary clattering
outside the door, as of three persons trying to ascend
abreast a flight of stairs only wide enough for one,
and quarrelling about the precedence, and in the
intervals of their emphatic remarks to each other
uttering cries of exultant triumph, as if they had
made some long-sought discovery, suddenly petrified
the various members into flesh and blood statues

with breeches on, and mouths open. Not long, however, did they remain thus inactive, for a mighty rush from the outside carried the door from its hinges, knocked Mr. Quackenbush, the stalwart guardian of the portal, into a far corner of the room, and disclosed to the astonished gaze of the assembled Elephantines, the forms of three individuals, to them unknown. The action of the Higholdboy, who first recovered his senses and his presence of mind, is worthy of remembrance. Keeping both eyes fixed upon one of the intruders, he deliberately drank the contents of his tumbler, and then, taking a cool aim, he threw the glass-ware at him. This act of the Higholdboy was regarded as an announcement, by implication, that crockery and glass-ware could be used on the present occasion offensively, and accordingly the other members followed the example of their chief. For a few minutes the destruction of property was great, and the more so, as, whenever a tumbler, plate, bottle, or any other similar missile fell to the floor unfractured, one of the three intruding parties would stamp on it with one of his feet, and pulverize it instanter. When the crockery was all disposed of, the assault was renewed with lemons, crackers, bologna sausages, and whatever projectiles remained, and the chairs and tables would have undoubtedly followed suit, had not the precaution previously taken, of chaining them up, precluded the possibility of their being used for this purpose. The result of this peculiar reception of the intruding parties was the temporary demolition of one, who had been hit over the head with the lemon-squeezer, and knocked down in the corner behind the chair of the Higholdboy. The second person had rolled himself up in a heap as well as he could, drew his head into his coat, and seemed resigned to whatever might be his fate. The third, however, made no resistance whatever, but rushed into one corner, turned his face to the wall, in which position he sustained for five minutes a brilliant cannonade of lemons, Boston crackers, with an occasional bomb in the shape of a nut-cracker and doughnut, for which affectionate tokens of respect he was indebted to the kindness of Van Dam, who bestowed upon him his undivided attention.

At the moment when the utter defeat of the invaders was shown to be a fixed fact, Johnny Cake reëntered the room. He saw the confusion which was everywhere apparent, and his first inquiry was as to the cause. Before he had been answered his eyes caught a sight of the party in the corner, who had ventured to turn his face around.

" Here," said Johnny, " you've got one of my railroad party, whose adventures I have detailed to you this evening."

" The devil !" said Spout.

" How unfortunate !" remarked Quackenbush.

" Are you seriously injured ?" asked Van Dam of the man in the corner, who was no other than Overdale.

" Nary time," was Overdale's response. " But where's Dennis ?" he asked.

" Here," said Dennis, as a head was seen to protrude from itself a coat-collar, like a tormented turtle from its shell, and, after some scrambling, Mr. Damon Dennis was erect and experimenting with his wooden leg, with the view of ascertaining whether it had suffered another fracture since the railroad experience.

Wagstaff also essayed forth from behind the capacious seat of the presiding dignitary of the club, and, after shaking the wrinkles out of himself, was once more himself.

Johnny Cake here introduced himself to the parties. They remembered him as having been one of the audience which listened to their free and easy concerts whilst travelling. They were then successively introduced to the different members of the club, all of whom expressed their regrets at having received them in so informal a manner, whilst Dennis, Overdale, and Wagstaff, protested that the apologies were useless, as they should not have made such an informal call. Mr. Spout again operated the telegraph for all parties, and when they were once more seated, Johnny Cake called on their uninvited guests for an explanation as to how they had found out their location. The statement was given by all three of the parties in disconnected sentences, sometimes one talking, and sometimes all. The narrations occupied about an hour in their delivery, and were replete with interest, but too long to be incorporated *verbatim* into these veracious records. The facts disclosed, however, were substantially these:

After leaving the steamboat, they made their way to the Shanghae Hotel, without loss of life or further limb. Each had his carpet-bag in his hand, and having made a demonstration towards the hall-door, the attendants came out to relieve them of their loads. Unused as they were to a reception of this kind, their greeting was rather peculiar than otherwise. Overdale put his hands on his pockets, and told *his* gentleman to clear out. Wagstaff, with great presence of mind, knocked *his* down instanter. Dennis started to run, but finding his wooden leg impeded his speed, sat flat down on the sidewalk and called for a constable. Being eventually satisfied that the intentions of the individuals were honorable, they went into the house and placed their names on the register; Overdale, who did not understand this last performance, expressing his surprise that they should be required to sign a note for their board as soon as they came into the house. They were shown to separate rooms, and each proceeded to make himself as comfortable as his limited know-

6

ledge of the uses of the bedroom furniture would
admit, preparatory to making his appearance in the
dining-room. They were all shown this latter part
of the establishment, after they had visited, arm-in-
arm, the barber's shop, the ladies' parlor, and the
hat-shop next door, in their vain search for something to eat.

As they entered the room, and the head waiter
approached, for the purpose of showing them some
seats, Overdale took his arm, and, having marched
the whole length of the room, was finally seated at
one end of the table, while his two companions were
accommodated with chairs immediately opposite.
Their exploits at their first dinner in the city were
many—being all of them ignorant of napkins, and
innocent of silver forks, their performances with those
unknown articles were something out of the common order.

Having recovered from their first impression, that
the bills of fare were religious tracts, left for the
spiritual improvement of the boarders, by the
Moral Reform Society, and having ascertained that
they were in some way connected with the science
of gastronomy, they proceeded to call for whatever
they imagined would suit their palates. Wagstaff
began with tarts, then taking a fancy to a jelly, he

reached for them, and devoured them all, seventeen in number; and concluded his dinner by eating a shad without picking out the bones.

Dennis, had somewhere heard of ice cream, for which frigid monstrosity he immediately called; when it came, not knowing exactly how to dispose of it, and perceiving that other people made use of the bottles from the caster-stand, he concluded that it would be proper to season his cream in like manner. He began with the pepper, followed it with vinegar, kept on to the Cayenne, added a good quantity of oil, drowned it with ketchup, and then with unusual impartiality, not wishing to neglect any of the bottles, he poured Worcestershire sauce over the whole. He eat it with the mustard-spoon and pronounced it excellent.

Overdale seeing a gentleman, on leaving the table, throw down his napkin, called to him across the room that he had dropped his handkerchief, and then with the consciousness of having done a neighborly turn, he proceeded to eat his dinner. He studied for some time over his own napkin, but eventually concluded that it would be proper to put it in his chair, so that he would not soil the cushion, and accordingly disposed of it in that manner, and sat down upon it with great care, for fear he should tear

it. He then opened his bill of fare at the wine-list,
and after puzzling for some time over the names, put
his finger in the middle, and told the waiter he
would " have some of that." The servant perceiving how matters stood, and having compassion on
his queer customer, brought him some soup. He at
once set to work to eat it with his fork, in which
attempt he scalded both his mouth and his fingers,
whereupon he drank the water in his finger-bowl
to cool his mouth, and wiped his fingers in his hair
to reduce their temperature. The considerate waiter
came once more to the rescue, and brought him some
beef, and also performed the same kindness for
Dennis, and probably saved him from absolute star-
vation. But Overdale, never remarkable for strict
temperance, looked for something to drink, and perceiving nothing that looked juicy, save the bottles in
the castor-stand, he took out one of them, and having
filled an egg-cup with the contents thereof, drank
it down. As it was salad oil, he did not feel disposed
to repeat the experiment. Having cleaned his nails
with a nut-pick, and pared an apple with a fish-slice,
he concluded his performances by putting half a
dozen fried oysters in his pocket and leaving the table.

At night they went immediately to bed, only finding their own rooms after poking their heads into

every other apartment on the same floor, and eventually securing the services of the chambermaid as a guide.

Overdale having got this lady to light his gas, was not able to get to bed without doing something further extraordinary, so wishing to open his window, he called a boy to his door twenty-seven times, by pulling at the bell-rope, which he imagined to be connected, in some inexplicable manner, with the sash. He was at last ready to go to sleep, when he blew out his gas, and laid down on the carpet, covering himself with the hearth-rug, fearing to get into the bed lest he should rumple the sheets. He woke up subsequently, and yelled for a waiter. One happened to be passing in the hall at that moment, and answered his call. Overdale asked where the tavern-keeper was, as he wanted too see him. He didn't want to be imposed upon, if he was from the country, and considered it a huge imposition to put a man into a room which was right over an asafœtida factory. The waiter comprehended the nature of Mr. Overdale's difficulty, and explained to him the nature of carburetted hydrogen, and the mistake that he had made in blowing out the light, instead of turning off the gas. Mr. Overdale thanked the waiter for his valuable information, and after waiting for the room to be well ventilated, he retired to rest—this time, however, in the bed, the waiter having kindly explained to him that the bed-clothing was nicely adjusted for the express purpose of being rumpled up, in order to give employment to a useful class of the community known as chambermaids.

In the morning, by one of those curious coincidences which we know do happen, but for which we cannot account, our three rural friends found themselves, at precisely eight o'clock, in the bar-room, before the bar, and calling upon the major for something to drink. Each drank, after which they went in to breakfast.

The bill of fare not being so complicated as the one on the dinner-table the day previous, and being printed in good readable English, they had no difficulty in procuring breakfast entirely to their satisfaction. After arising, and supplying themselves with cigars, they started out on an exploring expedition through the city.

Overdale, having read a good deal about the various "lions" of the town, assumed to know all about it, and therefore Dennis and Wagstaff acquiesced in his taking the lead; Wagstaff taking notes of everything for the benefit of his children when he returned home.

They strayed into Taylor's saloon, which Overdale informed them was the Crystal Palace. Gurney's Daguerreotype Gallery he stated was the American Art Union. The three then took the cars on the corner of Canal street and Broadway, Overdale remarking that he hoped all their lives were insured, as they were now on the Camden and Amboy Railroad. Dennis hoped they would run off the track in such a way that his wooden leg would be again broken. He would then retire for a few weeks, swear that he had lost a leg by the accident, sue the company for fifty thousand dollars damages, compromise by accepting ten thousand, and then go to Kansas and set up a faro bank. As they passed the Jefferson Market fire-alarm bell-tower, Overdale said it was a shot tower, erected in revolutionary times. They then arrived at the real Crystal Palace, which Overdale declared answered to the descriptions he had read of Fulton Market. The submarine armor which was on exhibition, he explained was a flying machine. The statue of the Amazon was noted down in Wagstaff's book, upon the authority of Overdale, as a cast-iron black foot squaw, on a prairie mustang. The fountain was announced to be a patent frog-pond. After writing down an accurate description of the fire-engines and hose-carts (the

[""]

...

first of which Overdale supposed to be perpetual self-acting locomotives, and the second a newly-invented threshing machine), Wagstaff proposed they should leave. The Croton Reservoir, Overdale stated was the gas-works. They then ascended the Latting Observatory, which their intelligent informant assured them was Trinity Church. From the altitude they here attained, they were favored with a view of a large extent of country. Overdale called the attention of his companions to the High Bridge over the Harlem river, of which they had an excellent view. He said that it was one of the few gigantic relics of the architecture of the Norsemen, whom he stated populated this country ten centuries before Columbus sculled over here in a scow-boat. This was the same bridge, he further remarked, which Edgar A. Hood, a historian, and an intimate friend of Nicholas Galileo, a poet of the sixteenth century, had spoken of as a "bridge of size." Mr. Overdale stated that the squadron of pleasure-yachts anchored at Hoboken were a number of clam-sloops, which had probably been abandoned by their owners, because they were old and unseaworthy. Jersey City, he was inclined to believe, from its general description and situation, was the Sixth Ward, which he further stated was in the centre of the Five Points. The

Penitentiary on Blackwell's Island, of which they had an excellent view, he informed them was the City Hall—the regular resort of the Common Scoundrels of the city. When they left the Observatory they strayed over into Avenue D, which, upon the word of the intelligent Overdale, Wagstaff described in his book as the Bowery. After mistaking the Dry Dock for the Battery, and a Williamsburg ferry boat for a Collins steamer, they continued to wander about, making divers mistakes, all of which were faithfully noted down as facts in Wagstaff's note-book. At eight o'clock in the evening, they found themselves in the Franklin Museum, whither they had gone on Overdale's invitation, to visit the Free Love Club. When the performance was over they sallied out, and fetched up in a German lager-bier saloon in William street, where the assembled Teutons were singing their national airs. For a moment Overdale was in doubt, but, after two minutes' thought, he informed his friends that they were in the Academy of Music, listening to an Italian Opera. When they left they were full of music, they having caught the inspiration from being in the presence of foreign artists, and immediately commenced to sing once more "Vilikins and his Dinah," with a strong chorius, but were almost immediately choked down

6*

by the police. They wandered about disconsolate, inquiring frequently of some hurrying passer-by where they could find the elephant, and receiving in reply to their interrogations a great variety of directions as to his whereabouts, from disinterested persons, all of which they noted down for reference. They searched an hour and a half for "my uncle, in the second story of the Fifth Avenue Railroad," which individual, they had been informed, could give them the desired information; they walked about four miles in search of "No. 1 'round the corner," at which place they had been assured, by a venerable female of Milesian accent who sold pea-nuts on the curb-stone, they would undoubtedly find the wished-for quadruped on exhibition. In the course of this latter search, as they were about to venture into a promising-looking saloon, for the purpose of procuring something to allay their thirst, Wagstaff caught a glimpse of the miniature elephant which was over the door of the club-room; and imagining that he had discovered the veritable animal, he uttered a cry of joy which attracted his companions to the same object, upon which they made a grand rush up the flight of stairs. Where they got to, and how they were received, is already told.

When the narrative had been concluded, Mr. John

Spout, the Higholdboy of the club, declared in
solemn terms, that, by virtue of his office, the three
persons whose adventures had just been related by
themselves should be henceforth considered members of the Elephantine order. He added that any
member might object if he chose, but it wouldn't do
him any good, as he should immediately overrule
the objection, and kick the daring objector down
stairs.

This persuasive manner of addressing the members
had the desired effect. They were convinced by the
gentle logic of their dignified superior officer, and
they could not have the heart to oppose him had
they felt so inclined.

Messrs. Wagstaff, Overdale, and Dennis, who
were thus so summarily promoted, were solemnly
sworn in on a boiled ham, after which all hands
joined in singing, "We won't go home till morning." It may be proper to add, in respect to this
last musical asseveration, and as a deserved tribute to
the veracity of the persons concerned, that when they
said they wouldn't go home till morning, *they didn't.*

The Colored Camp-Meeting.

There is a divinity that shapes our ends,
Rough——

                                                                SHAKSPEARE.

An evening or two after the facts related in the last chapter of this veritable and never-to-be-believed history, the members of the club were seated in silent deliberation round their table, each man smoking a short pipe by a special order of the council; an unusual commotion was noticed at the end of the table where John Spout was supposed to be anchored. First the smoke, which had settled, in a thick, hazy layer, upon everything, and concealed the members from each other, as if they had mutually

129

pulled the wool over each other's eyes until all were for a time invisible, was observed to wave to and fro, as if agitated by some powerfully moving cause, concealed from the observers by the fragrant tobacco fog which had been raised by the joint exertions of the assembled multitude. A few minutes more disclosed the arm of John Spout, working like an insane windmill, backwards and forwards, to open a clear space, and make himself visible to the naked eye.

After the lapse of some little time, and the expenditure of no small amount of muscular power in this interesting exercise, the ruddy beef-face of the Higholdboy beamed forth from the encircling mist, like a good-natured light-house, which had been on a spree the night before, and got up with a red nose, in consequence of the nocturnal dissipation. As soon as he had cleared a space about him large enough for him to speak without danger of suffocation, he announced that he had a proposition to lay before the honorable body, and proceeded to state that he had observed in a morning paper an advertisement of a camp-meeting, to be held at a distance from the city easily accessible, by a 2′40″ team, in a couple of hours. He, moreover, went on to say, that the presiding officers of the gospel-hunt were to be of a sable complexion, and that the greater part of the

congregation was expected to be of the same color—
in fact, it was to be what a Bowery boy would, in
his peculiar, but not inexpressive dialect, call a
" Nigger Methodist Camp Meeting." The proposition of the pious Mr. Spout was that the Elephants
should pack their pockets, and proceed to the scene
of action, for the purpose of picking up any superfluous piety that might be lying around loose, and
of making themselves generally agreeable, and having a good time all round.

The suggestion was listened to with approval, and
it was unanimously

Resolved, that the Elephants proceed to the camp-
ground in the morning.

A special committee, consisting of the entire club,
was appointed to see that every person was provided
with all the necessaries of life, and the requisites for
having a juicy time.

In consideration of his being the mover of the
scheme, it was moved that J. Spout, Esq., should be
empowered to procure from the livery-stable the
necessary conveyances, and should become person-
ally responsible for the same.

The proposition was agreed to, with a clause to
the effect that when he paid the bill he should treat
the company with the change.

Each man then appointed every other man a committee to raise the means, and keep himself sober until the appointed hour, after which they adjourned to prepare.

At eight, by the City Hall clock (and, of course, half-past eight by every other clock in the city) next morning, the convention was incomplete.

For an hour there were three men lacking; but Mr. John I. Cake finally made his appearance, with his breeches tucked into his boots, a horsewhip in his hand, and a suspicious-looking protuberance immediately over his left coat pocket. The attention of the company being called to this, Johnny explained by saying that it was his Testament and hymn-book, and that he had been all the morning engaged in turning down the leaves at the proper places, so that he might not be interrupted in his devotions. A half hour longer was appropriated in waiting for Wagstaff and Overdale, but at the end of that time, those two worthies failing to appear, the party resolved to start without them, Boggs remarking, that if those tardy individuals failed to reach Heaven because of their religious shortcomings, they could not say, in extenuation of their offence, that their fraternal Elephants had not waited a sufficient time to give them an opportunity for salvation.

The vehicles provided for the occasion were two single buggies, into which all seven of the party were to pack themselves, a feat which was finally accomplished, much to the detriment of Johnny Cake's shirt-collar, and greatly to the discomfiture of Quackenbush, who had to sit in behind, and let his legs hang over.

Van Dam took the reins of the foremost carriage, and his first exploit was to run the wheel against the curbstone, and spill the party into a coal-hole, from which they were rescued by the exertions of the bystanders. They once more started on their journey, under the supervision of Quackenbush, who was recalled from the stern of the craft, and made to assume the guidance of the crazy horse.

Van Dam, on being deprived of his charge, immediately went to sleep, and waked no more, except when his companions roused him to pay the toll, which they did at every gate, until there was no more small change in his pockets than there is gunpowder in a tom-cat, after which they offered to pay every time with a twenty-dollar bill, and as no one would assume the responsibility of changing it, they passed free, and proceeded merrily enough until they reached the encampment of the devout darkeys.

There being no taverns immediately adjoining, the

horses were made as comfortable as circumstances would admit of, under a beech-tree, in a clover-field, and the human part of the Elephantine delegation marched in an exceedingly irregular procession to the camp ground; the line of march being occasionally thrown into disorder by John Spout, who persisted in making protracted and strenuous efforts to squeeze something wet out of a Schiedam schnapps bottle, which had been dry as a powder-horn ever since Quackenbush had his last pull at it.

A description of the sylvan scene which met their metropolitan gaze may not be out of place.

It was in a clearing, in a piece of beech and maple woods. Stands were erected for some of the prominent speakers; slabs were laid from stump to stump, for the accommodation of such of the brothers and sisters as desired to sit still and listen to the preaching, and in places straw was laid on the ground, for the special benefit of such as had the "power," and wanted to get down on the ground and have a private tussle with the devil on their own account. Stands were erected under the trees, in the shadiest spots, by enterprising white folks, for the sale of gingerbread and root-beer, and it was rumored that some speculators, distrusting the appearance of the "sperits of just men made perfeck," had supplied their place with other spirits, full as potent and equally reliable.

The grass might have been agreeable to look upon at a distance, but a close inspection showed it to be full of pismires; the stumps would have been commodious seats, if they had not been most of them previously appropriated by black-snakes; the sleeping places would have been tents, if they had not been huts, and a poetical fancy might have pictured them as being constructed of canvas, white as the driven snow, but the practical mind instantly discovered that they were made of oak slabs and dirty horse-blankets. Some imaginative people would have set down the speaking of the ministers as eloquence if not inspiration, but a critical individual would have found fault with the bad grammar, and insinuated that the inspiration was all perspiration.

At the north end of the ground, a big darkey in his shirt-sleeves was mounted on a platform, preaching to a crowd, who seemed, by their vermicular contortions, to be possessed of a legion of eely devils. On the west side, a fat wench was stirring up the fire under a big kettle of soup, seemingly composed principally of onions and ham; in a sly corner a red-shirt b'hoy was displaying the mysterious evolu-

tions of the "little joker," and two small specimens
of ebony juvenility were playing euchre on a basswood log ; opposite to these, mounted on a cider barrel, a molasses-colored gentleman was going through
a rather extraordinary performance; he had preached
till his audience had all left him; then shouted
" Hallelujah," and " Glory," till he was hoarse ; had
sung hymns in a spasmodic whisper till his voice
gave entirely out, and now, in despair at being
unable to speak, yet compelled to work off his
superabundant religion, as if he were a locomotive
with too big a head of steam on, he was dancing on
one leg, and kicking the other about in a kind of perpetual pigeon-wing, and tossing his arms upwards in
a wild and original manner, as if he was using his
utmost endeavors to climb to heaven on an invisible
tarred rope.

To the shouts of the men, and the screams of the
women who had got too much religion, was added
the laughter of the outsiders, who hadn't got enough
religion, and the swearing of the gamblers, who
hadn't got any religion; and to complete the harmony, from a neighboring pasture was wafted the
roars of a herd of cattle, applauding, in their own
peculiar manner, an extemporaneous bull-fight.

Mr. Dropper gave it as his opinion, that camp-meeting religion, if analyzed, would be found to consist of equal parts of rum, rowdyism, and insanity. As, however, it was deemed improper to decide without a complete examination of the premises, it was resolved to proceed in company to explore the place.

Quackenbush, who had resumed his nap on the grass, was roused, and after getting the grasshoppers out of his hair, the sand-flies out of his ears, and pulling off his boots to look for centipedes, he was declared ready for active duty, and they proceeded on their march.

They found in a side hut of more pretentious appearance than the rest, that there was something unusual going on, and upon inquiring, discovered that one of the fragrant flock having transgressed, he was then having his trial before the "session."

The party moved on to where the minister in his shirt-sleeves was edifying a small, but select, not to say noisy, congregation. The audience seemed to be affected much in the same manner as a strong shock of electricity will stir up a crowd of boys who have all got hold of the same wire. As there seemed to be a prospect of fun, the Elephants made a temporary halt to witness the same.

The sermon was now concluded, and the shirt-sleeve-man kneeled down on the platform and began to pray; he must have had no inconsiderable amount of similar exercise before, for the knees of his pantaloons were worn entirely through, and there was a large hole behind where he had sat upon his heels.

No sooner had he fairly commenced praying than some of the more energetic in the crowd began to groan; when he made a thorny point, and said something about the "arrow of conviction," some fat wench would sing out "Glory;" when he put in a touch about hell fire and other torrid climates, they would cry out "Yes, Lord." And when he put in an extra lick about repentance, and death, and damnation, and other pleasant luxuries, the whole crowd fairly screamed with excitement.

At length a powerful darkey, with a head like a cord of No. 1 curled hair, and with nothing on to hide his black anatomy but a pair of thin breeches and a blue shirt, began to give unequivocal manifestations of the workings of his faith; first he kicked a woman with his right leg, then he kicked a little boy with his left, then he punched one of the brethren in the stomach, then he stepped on the toes of a grey-haired class-leader, but, as both were barefooted, no harm was done ; then he yelled like seven Indians, and howled like seven Irishmen, and danced about like a whole regiment of crazy Dutchmen. When he opened his mouth, the minister dodged the yawning chasm, and the man fell down and sprawled about in the mud, striking about with his arms and legs, as if he were swimming on a bet, and was only two minutes from the stake-boat. At last he ceased to move, and stiffened out as if he had suddenly swallowed a rifle-barrel, which stuck in his throat like Macbeth's amen. The damaged brethren gathered round ; the sisters, after giving their injured shins a consoling rub, also came to the rescue, and the man was picked up. He was foaming at the mouth ; his teeth were set together so that a fence-stake was required to pry them apart ; his shirt was unbuttoned (his pantaloons had unbuttoned themselves) ; a pailful of water out of the nearest frog-pond was dashed in his face, and he soon so far recovered himself as to ask for corn whisky. All immediately sang, with a strong chorus, a thanks-giving hymn, that his soul was saved ; though what connection there was between corn whisky and salvation puzzled the Elephantines some, if not more.

When this interesting episode in the day's performance was concluded, the participants picked themselves up, and prepared to again besiege Satan in his stronghold, the north side of Sebastopol of the hearts of sinful niggers. Singing was the first feature, and the hymn was of a style unique, and, to the Elephants, highly refreshing. In point of comparison they had never known anything like it, and the execution was incomparable to anything known to exist by them. An athletic colored individual sang the words of the hymn, and, after each verse, the whole congregation would join in the swelling chorus.

The effect of the hymn was electric. No less than twenty-seven colored females were seized with spasmodic religion, whilst over a dozen of the sterner sex found themselves unable to longer resist the thirsting of the spirit for religious nourishment, and they, too, fell over, and, amid the howling, kicking, singing, shouting and indescribable confusion that followed, Mr. Quackenbush expressed it as his opinion that chaos had come.

But Mr. Boggs was seriously affected by the performance. He fell down in the grass, and laughed, and rolled, and positively refused to be comforted or get up, until the rest of the company ran sticks in his ears, and put last year's chestnut-burs down his

back. When he had sufficiently recovered, the
members of the club renewed their investigations.
They listened to several exhortations and hymns,
and then peeped under the horse-blanket tents. In
one they saw a youthful wench, trying to pray with
her mouth full of cold sausage. Her efforts were
useless, and becoming satisfied of this fact herself,
she concluded, very sensibly, to no longer try to save
her soul on an empty stomach, but see to her bodily
wants first. Before she had got ready to pray again
she had drank a pint of gin, which so heightened her
religious enthusiasm that she made a dive among
the pious elders, gave four shouts of glory, and fell
into the arms of a venerable gentleman, who divided
his time for the next hour in kissing the young
sister, and crying amen and glory in alternation.

At last, the Elephants concluded to return to the
city. They piled themselves into the vehicles, and
by means of sundry persuasive arguments, the horses
were induced to reach the livery-stable, rather
warm, inside of two hours.

After the party had stowed away divers beef-
steaks and onions, and other articles of food, they
ascended into the club-room. Here they found
Overdale and Wagstaff, both asleep. They were
awakened, and, in a peremptory manner, the High-

oldboy demanded to know why they had not been on hand in the morning at the place of rendezvous, to witness the sable performance in the rural districts. The answers of the two offending individuals differed. Wagstaff assigned as a reason that he was asleep, whereas Overdale stated that he wasn't awake. The Higholdboy announced himself satisfied with the answers.

Further Discoveries.

"There is a tide in the affairs of men,
Which taken at the flood leads on ——"

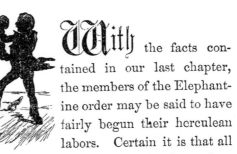 **With** the facts contained in our last chapter, the members of the Elephantine order may be said to have fairly begun their herculean labors. Certain it is that all the spare time they could command was devoted to an investigation into the particular speciality in zoölogical science, for which the club had been organized; and certain it is that the prospect of some rare contribution from members at the next regular meeting was good.

The meeting night arrived at length, the members were all present, and punctual to the hour.

The Higholdboy had brought with him a pair of boxing-gloves, which he announced were to be used in this wise: He was determined to keep order in the meetings, and this, too, even if he had to resort to severe means to do so. But actuated by the same feelings of benevolence which animated the legislators who caused the passage of laws to prevent cruelty to animals, he did not want to do physical injury to the refractory members of the club. Therefore, he had brought the aforesaid boxing-gloves, so that when he knocked a member down, he wouldn't either draw blood or give him a black eye.

This humane considerateness on the part of Mr. Spout was warmly commended by the brethren, and Mr. Quackenbush, in behalf of the club,

Resolved, that the Higholdboy is a model presiding officer.

This resolution in behalf of the club was adopted by Mr. Quackenbush.

Overdale here arose and said that he fully coincided with the spirit of the resolution; he had a proposition to make, however, which was to order up some cold corned beef, celery, mustard, rolls, and butter, provided he would consent to let the members keep order after their own fashion.

This appeal to Mr. Spout's feelings was irresistible,

and he gave his full consent, saying that that was all
he had contemplated under any circumstances, and
if they could ring in Overdale for the feed, it was so
much gained. It was accordingly ordered that
Overdale give his order.

Mr. Boggs said that boxing-gloves forcibly re-
minded him of some experience he had had several
years previously. Though a person by no means
thin, and notwithstanding the fact that he had been
for years troubled with chronic good health, yet,
from reading at that time various physiological works,
he had become convinced, that from the want of
proper physical training, his dissolution might be
considered near at hand, unless he took immediate
measures to save his precious life by means of active
exercise. He accordingly visited the gymnasiums,
but the idea of putting himself into such fantastic
shapes as he saw young men doing, was to him not
to be thought of. Further, he was decidedly opposed
to the idea of making himself the laughing-stock of
a set of young rascals by his awkward efforts in his
incipient progress. Whilst he was yet undecided, a
friend suggested to him that he procure a couple of
pairs of boxing-gloves, and practise with them. "Having purchased the gloves," continued Mr. Boggs,
"I was still at a loss to know how to proceed. I didn't

want to practice with anybody, because I knew that my awkwardness would make mirth for them, and to this I was decidedly opposed. Under these circumstances I resorted to other means. In the garret of the house in which I lived was a mammoth stove —in fact, gentlemen, a stove which I could strike and not knock over, which would not laugh at me in my attacks, and therefore a stove with which I made up my mind to have a few rounds each day.

"The next day I went up into the garret. There stood the sable champion of heavy weight, and, for the first time in my life, I stripped myself of my coat, to fight without being appalled. The stove loomed up in giant proportions; I stood before it, and squared off as well as I knew how. I imagined I saw the stove's right fist coming at my left eye. I parried off the blow, which, without, doubt would have been aimed at me, had the stove had a right fist as I imagined, and with my right fist I planted a stunner in the place where his bread-basket should have been. The result was a powerful reaction, and I found myself sprawling on the floor. I ascertained that I was not damaged, and wisely determined then that I would not strike such powerful blows in the future.

"I again squared off, and began putting in the

blows in rapid succession, whilst I managed success-
fully to keep my adversary from hitting me in even
one of the many attempts which I imagined he
made. I kept up the practice about an hour.

"The next day I resumed my practice, and I kept
it up for several weeks, when I fancied that I was
sufficiently expert to 'travel on my muscle.'

"To be sure, I had fought an inanimate object,
which could not strike; still, in the tussles I had
imagined the stove striking at me from all conceiv-
able directions, and I had not only been able to
guard-off these imaginary blows, but I had shown the
stove that I could put in a few astonishers between
times.

"I was ready now for practice with a living adversary. But who was he to be? that was the question.
I was still unwilling to call in any of my acquaintances, as I might possibly after all be found *veni*, *vidi*,
vici, as we say in the classics, which, when translated
into English, means weighed in the balance and
found short (suppressed snickers).

"One day, as I was cogitating upon the matter in
front of the house, a big nigger, full six feet in height,
came along. He looked as if he wanted a job, and
with a good deal of trepidation, I ventured to ask
him if I was right in supposing him anxious to make
a half-dollar. I found him to be an eager candidate

for any position, from a cashier of a bogus bank up to a boot-black. I took him up in the garret and disclosed to him the nature of my desires, and took occasion to inform him that I would give him a half-dollar for two hours services per day, and a quarter in addition never to say a word about the matter; to this he assented, and I told him to put on the gloves. He took the dirty pair out of respect to me (not taking into consideration the probable consequence to me, in case of his succeeding in putting in a few licks), and I took the clean pair.

" We squared off, and occupied a minute or two in preliminary practice; I felt fully confident that I could manage him quite as easily as I had the stove, and after telling him to do his best, I proceeded to give him a poke in his breast. We gradually warmed in the work, the blows passed more frequently, and as we proceeded I became conscious of the fact that I managed to put in almost one blow to his three. I then made my calculations to give the nigger a regular rib riser, and just as I was about to consummate this well digested plan, I became apprised that something important had happened; what it was I was unable for a minute or two to decide; several thoughts passed rapidly through my mind. One idea I had was, that a bombshell from Sebastopol had exploded in the identical premises which I was then occupying. But this gave way to another, which was that New York had been tipped over into Buttermilk Channel; then again, I thought that somebody was using my head for a rattle-box; several other theories suggested themselves to me, all of which were equally reasonable. But at anyrate the cause of the peculiar sensations was soon solved. The nigger had given me a clip, covering the lower part of my proboscis, my mouth, and chin, had set my nose bleeding, and cut my lips somewhat against my teeth, and the blood was flowing profusely.

"I looked around for the nigger, but he had disappeared; the probability is that he thought he had been the cause of my death, and fearing an indictment for murder, had vamosed without stopping to get his fifty cents.

"I picked myself up as well as I could, and travelled down stairs to my room. A look into the

mirror presented to my view an interesting picture of myself; not only were my nose and lips swollen, but the gloves which the nigger had on, being blackened with the stove-blacking, had communicated the metallic polish to my face and shirt, so that both were of a beautiful sheet-iron color. I kept my room for ten days; sent word to the landlady that I had the measles, and requested that nobody be admitted to my room but the servant who brought me my food, and him I feed liberally to keep mum. When I got well enough to go out, I loaned my boxing gloves to a young gentleman, with my mind fully made up that if he never offered to return them, I shouldn't send a constable after him, nor ask him for them. I have not indulged in any amusements of the kind since, and I am glad to announce that I am fully satisfied with my past experience in the study of the science."

Mr. Boggs's narrative was loudly applauded. He, however, protested against the civility.

Mr. Van Dam characterized it as a valuable contribution, which called forth from Mr. Boggs the question, " What the devil he meant by calling it a contribution; he had no idea of the kind."

The members insisted that, however he might regard it, it certainly was a valuable contribution to their entertainment, and would grace the archives of the club.

Mr. Boggs stated that had he entertained the most distant idea he was doing anything of any value to anybody, he should have never been able

7*

to say a word.   If it was a contribution he was glad
of it.

The Higholdboy then called upon the other members for their contributions to science.

Mr. Quackenbush responded, and after drinking
some Croton water diluted with gin, he began :

"Last evening I started out on a cruise, with the
view of seeing the elephant on the streets by gas-
light.   I saw the identical elephant to be seen every
evening, and with which you are all familiar, and I
began to think about eleven o'clock that I should be
compelled to retire to rest without having seen anything worthy of note.   To be sure, I had seen a fight
between a nigger and Irishman, which, after the first
round, was finished by each party running away as
fast as his legs could carry him, thereby tacitly
acknowledging that he was beaten ; but what was
this ?   Every one of you have been in fights, and of
course it would be unnatural to suppose that a description of a scrimmage of brief duration between
an Irishman and a nigger would be particularly interesting.   I was about to turn my footsteps homeward,
when the movements of an individual attracted my
attention.   The person in question was a gentleman of
about forty-five years of age.   His height was fully
six feet, his form was very spare, his face thin, his

nose sharp and prominent, his eyes and hair grey, and his face closely shaven, wrinkled, and sallow. He was dressed in a plain black dress-coat and pants, of a style about three years old. His vest was of black satin, his shirt-bosom was scrupulously white; a black silk choker was tightly enveloped about his neck, above which peered a diminutive collar, which, when it was put on, was without doubt a standing-collar, but the starch had not been made of such a consistency as to render it consistent for the collar to stand up against the unstiffening effects of a hot day's sweating. As I saw him, he was coming down the street at a rapid rate, describing all sorts of geometrical figures on the sidewalk, and making efforts to sing the words of "Yankee Doodle" to the tune of "Old Hundred." Whenever he ran against an awning-post, he would stop, and expostulate with the post for its want of civility, and would insist that the post had never been born and bred in the St. Lawrence country, or it would have shown more politeness to strangers. He was entirely unable to account for the sudden revolutions of the earth, which made day and night follow each other in such quick succession. When he ran against a lamp-post, he would look up to the light and insist that it was dinner-time, and would wonder why the old woman didn't blow the horn.

At that moment a policeman came along, and was going to take him into custody. On observing the policeman's uniform, he inquired of him whether he was a 'Merican or British soger, and whether the Russians had whipped Nicholas, and whether Cuba had begun to bombard General Pierce at Sebastopol. I knew the officer very well, and he suggested that as the man seemed to be quite respectable in his appearance, it might be well to take him to a hotel for the night. I volunteered to do this, and accordingly took him under my care. On going down, he asked me if I was a karvern teeper, as he wanted to take a drink of bed, and then go to sleep on a blass of grandy. I told him I was, and would see him put to bed all right. On asking him his name, I learned that he was Deacon Josiah Pettingill, of St. Lawrence county. We got to the hotel, and I informed the clerk that the gentleman was a country friend of mine, whom I wanted stowed away for the night, and for whom I would call in the morning. I accompanied him to the room, assisted in removing his garments, and, after putting him between the sheets, I left the premises. This morning I called on him at his room, and found him still asleep. I proceeded to awaken him. It occupied some minutes to explain to him the true condition of affairs. At last, the whole

of the occurrences of the previous evening seemed
to come to his recollection.

"He inquired his condition when I found him. I
told him that he was at that time considerably drunk,
and disposed to be somewhat noisy.

"'Well, squire,' said he, 'I shouldn't be surprised
if it was so; the fact is, my head aches at this
minute as if it was ready to bust, and it feels jest as
it did once in my lifetime, a good while ago, when I
took too much egg nogg; that was full twenty-five
year ago; for awhile, I felt as if I was ridin' to.
Heaven over glairy ice down a high hill, on a bob-
sled with its runners greased. But I never got there;
I know one thing sartain—a few hours afterward I
felt as if the bob-sled had run agin a stump, when
almost tu the bottom of the hill, and the concussion
had landed me intu a cauldron-kettle full of fever and
ager and blacksmiths' hammers, mixed together in
equal parts; it wasn't funny, squire; I went right
off and jined the church, and hain't been blue since,
unless I wos last night.'

"I asked Mr. Pettingill to give me a history of his
experience in the city. He complied, and stated the
facts as follows :—

"'Well, you see, squire, I come to the city last
evenin' from Albany, in the railroad, and when I

got tu the shed where the railroad stops, I got out.
A feller stepped up tu me as important as a bantam
cock after he has crowed for the first time, and asked
me where I wanted tu go. I told him I wanted tu
go tu a first-rate tarvern. He said that idea was
ridiculous; that they never allowed distinguished
strangers tu go tu tarverns, and, unless he was mistaken, I was something above the common folks from
the rooral deestricts. I told him I was supervisor of
the town where I was born and brought up, in the
St. Lawrence country. He said he was thunderin'
glad to hear it, as he himself was something of a
high cockalorum of New York. He insisted upon
my gittin' intu the carriage and goin' tu his private
dwellin', as it would be vulgar tu go tu tarverns. I
asked him if the St. Nicholas Hotel was common.
He said that nobody but those that wasn't no great
shakes went there. We finally come tu a real big,
purty stun house, and the man jumped off from the
carriage. He told me again that if he was rich he
wasn't proud, and it was a way he had of always
ridin' outside and drivin'. I told him I always done
so, only in the consarn I had they all rode outside,
for the reason that there warn't no inside. With
that he larfed, and said that all folks didn't have jest
the same way of doin' things, and we went tu the

door. A nigger come and opened the door, and we
went in. There was about twenty gentlemen, fixed off
tu kill, and a table sot with bottles, and everything as
slickery as could be. The man who brought me took
me tu a fine-looking gentleman and told me that he
was his brother, that he was obleeged tu go out on
business connected with his office, but that he would
be back by 11 o'clock; he said his brother would
see tu me, and do the scrumptious while he was gone;
well, we set down tu the table; he was orful kind, for
he helped me tu everything he could on the table—
all kinds of chicken-fixens and ginger-bread arrangements; he then asked me tu take a glass of wine; I
told him I was a little tew much of a temperance
man for that; he said certainly he wouldn't ask me
if I had any scrooples agin' it; he asked me if I
was opposed to drinkin' cider; I said no, if it was
sweet; he said that they had got in, about a week
before, a barrel of sweet cider, which had jest enough
snap in it tu make it taste good; he told the nigger
tu take a bottle of wine up stairs tu his sick nephew,
and tu bring a pitcher full of cider up stairs from
the new barrel; the nigger left with the bottle and
the pitcher, and in about five minutes came back
intu the room with the pitcher full of the slickest
cider I ever seen; I drunk some of it, and it tasted

so good that I drunk more; when I had taken almost
enough, the gentleman asked me tu go into the back
room where a lot of men was a setting around a
table, holdin' little round pieces of bone in their hands
and puttin' 'em down, and another man was fum-
blin' with some pieces of paper; I asked him if they
wasn't playin' cards, 'cause I thought they looked as
if they was; he said no, that they was Wall street
stock-dealers, and that the pieces of bone stood for
so many shares of stock; he asked if I wouldn't like
tu become a stock-jobber, and he said there was a
power of money tu be made at the business; I said
I guessed not, but he seemed tu be anxious tu do a
little at it himself, and he asked me to lend him a
hundred dollars which he would give back tu me
when his brother came; after he had give me three
or four more glasses of cider, which, by this time, he
poured out of bottles, I handed him my money-puss
and told him tu help himself; he opened it and took
out all there was in it, which was ten dollars; he
asked me if that was all I had got, and I told him
that my calculations had been jest right; that when
I started from hum I had an idee that I should land
with jest ten dollars in my puss; he then asked me
if I had brought any checks or drafts, and I told
him no; so he said he would borrow the ten,

and he went into the stock business pretty heavy, and I watched to see how he made in the speculation, but after takin' three or four more glasses of that cider, I kinder lost the run of the speculation; he then said it would be a good idee tu go out and get some fresh air, which we did, after taking a little more of that cider; as we went along the streets, I thought that we didn't have tu move our feet—that the street moved up and down tu save us the trouble; the houses kinder got to playin' blind man's buff, and the streets got to heaving up and down orfully, and when I was wonderin' what on airth made it, I missed the gentleman; that, squire, is about all I recollect; but the fun of the matter is this, that I was cute enough not tu tell the gentleman I had three hundred dollar bills tucked behind the strap of my boot, in the leg.'

" Mr. Pettingill then took one of his boots from the floor, drew out the three hundred dollar bills, and held them up as a triumph of St. Lawrence cuteness.

" 'Now,' said he, 'squire, I want you tu show me a tarvern where nobody won't want tu borrow money of me. I am a little 'spicious of that man's brother. I don't believe he intended to pay me.'

"I told him that his present quarters were as desirable, in all points of view, as any he could find in the

city, after which I informed him, much to his astonishment, that he had been taken to a gambling-house,
and it was owing to his 'cuteness,' which, it seems,
did not forsake him when drunk, that he had not
lost all his money.

"Mr. Pettingill thanked me for the part I had taken
in his behalf, and gave me a pressing invitation to
come to his place in St. Lawrence county, next summer, and spend a month with him, all of which I
promised to do, if it was possible."

Mr. Quackenbush was congratulated on his good
fortune in coming across that particular species of
the elephant, whose nature and characteristics he
had so happily and correctly delineated in his paper.

It was moved by Mr. Dropper that a copy of the
contribution be requested from Quackenbush, to
make cigar-lighters of, and that the original be deposited in the big room of the American Institute, as a
specimen of bad chirography.

Mr. Q. said he would see them blowed first.

Mr. Van Dam next proceeded with his contribution :

"A few evenings since," said he, "as I was passing through one of the streets of Gotham, I observed
a crowd collected near a corner grocery. Thinking
that an opportunity.was afforded to see something

worth taking a note of, I ran for the spot in time to
see the difficulty. I found there a man, holding
with each hand a boy, and both of the juveniles
making frantic efforts to release themselves from his
grasp. The man was a small, cadaverous-appearing
individual, a compound of gamboge and chalk, the
gamboge predominating. There was a tinge of yellow in his face, he had yellow hair, and he had on a
suit of summer clothes, made of some yellow material. Nature had favored him with a dwarfed moustache, composed of twenty-eight yellow hairs, and
also an incipient beard, made up of seventy-six yellow hairs, and turned out in the shape of a triangle,
the base of which rested upon the chin, at the point
where it begins to retreat, and the apex of which
reached the middle of his under lip.

" The appearance of the boys would indicate that
they were of Irish birth. One had a squint-eye and
a head of hair which the youth of America are
accustomed to designate as a ' brick-top.' His snub
nose was ordinarily directed to an imaginary point
in the heavens, about forty-five degrees above the
horizon. His garments were not altogether the style
which would be pronounced *au fait*, by a Broadway
leader of the fashion. It would seem that he had
only one purpose in view in jumping into the afore-

said garments, which purpose was, not to create a
sensation, either by the accuracy of their fit, or the
newness of the material, but rather to cover his form,
and keep out the cold, at such times as the clerk of
the weather was induced to fetch up " heated terms "
all standing, and give us a specimen of the temperature, perhaps somewhat mollified, which is supposed
to exist in the immediate vicinity of Symmes Hole.
The description of one of the boys will do very well
for the other, except that in some particulars he was
a little more so, and in others a little less, which
statement, gentlemen, I consider sufficiently definite
for all practical purposes.

" The sympathies of the bystanders seemed to be
decidedly in favor of the boys, who were so violent
in their resistance that the man could hold them
only with great difficulty. Once they tripped him,
and then all three fell over a barrel of turnips, upsetting a barrel-cover containing apples ; but the man
was enabled to continue his hold on the boys. At
last, when one of them, by tangling his leg around
the man, upset him into a tub of pickles, the man
called out, in a shrill voice, ' Vatch ! vatch !' All
this transpired amid the shouts of the lookers-on.
' Go in, blinky,' said one. ' Keep a going, sour
krout,' said another; and various were the remarks

of this character which were heard. But, as usual, the police were not at hand, and the sequel proved that their absence was rather to be desired than otherwise. Notwithstanding the fact that the sympathies of the crowd were apparently in favor of the boys, yet the general feeling seemed to be that the merits of the case should be understood, and when the boys made an effort to escape, they were prevented; and when the vanquished German had extricated himself from the pickle-tub, one of the persons asked what the boys had done.

" 'Do,' said the grocery-keeper, ' dey do so much as to sends dem to de States brison. Dey is de vorst poys as runs in de shtreets. De oder night dey comes here to mine shtore-crocery a koople of times, and ven I vas not see dem, dey ketch my cats by de dails, and dies vire-crackers to de cat's dail, on de shtep-valk, and den sets vire to de crackers, and trows de cats down. Den de cats she runs like de tuyvel into de shtore so much scare. She yump all around on de counters, over into de barrels, breaks into bieces some new bottles vat I buy yust, sets vire to some paper vat vas lay on de counters, tumbles over ebery dings vat vas in de vay, and gets all shplitter shplatter mixed up togedder. I find some shweet oil bottles shpill in de box fon green dea; she knock down fom de shelf a big match-box, vich hold a gross fon matches, and dey go off and shmell so vorse mit primstone as if de tuyvel had moved into mine shtore-crocery, and I can't tell you so much damage as it do ; and ven I look for de cats, I find her about an hour rolled up in a pasket fon green beas, mit all de hair scorch off de pehind side fon her. Dis vas on Saturday night vill be two veeks.'

" 'Why didn't you catch them then ?' asked one of the party.

" 'Ketch dem,' said the grocery-man ; 'pefore I vas get over mine scare, dey vas run avay, and you might yust so vell try to find a needle mit a hay-shtacks as to find dem. But I tells de constopples about dem, and dey say dey vill look out for dem. Vell, two tree days go by, and von morning I comes down shtairs to unlocks de door fon mine shtore-cro-cery. De key vas in de inside de door, and ven I durns dem round to unlock dem yust, I hears some-dings shoot off on de oder side de door. I vas much scare, and I runs up shtairs, for I dinks some feller vants to shoot me, and I sends my vife out de oder door to look round on de shtep-valk, and see who vas dere. Ven she come back she say der bin no beeples dere, and so I go vonce more to unlocks de door. I durns de key so quick as I can, ven pop!

crack! shoot! I hears again de noise. I vas so much scare dat I falls over, and I bulls de door open. Ven I finds I vas not shoot, I looks in de lock and finds dere some bieces baper, vat you make de little vite vire-crackers—you call'——

"'Torpedoes,' suggested one of the persons present.

"'Yes, dorpedoes,' resumed the German, 'dat's the name.'

"'How do you know these boys put torpedoes in your lock?' asked one.

"'I know it so vell as I vants to know,' was the response.

"'Did you see 'em do it, or did anybody else? was the next question.

"'No, I did not see dem do it, but I know it was dem I can, shvear it vas dem,' said the confident accuser.

"'Pretty good swearin',' said a man in a red shirt. 'Say, old sour krout,' he continued, 'what else have the boys done?'

"'Mine Gott!' said the corner grocery-man, despairingly, 'is dat not enough vat I have tell you? Ven I go out my shtore-crocery for a minute, vonce dey durns de shpiggot fon de lager bier and vinegar parrells, and dey runs out in de floor and vaste; ven dey see me in de shtreets dey calls me ' *Old nicht's*

cum araus, sour kraut, sprech Deutsch.' Dey finds
dead rats, and trows dem on mine awning till dey
shmells so bad; dey brings an old barber's pole, and
sets dem up before mine shtore-crocery, on vich vas
paint, 'shaving done here,' and ven de beeples see
de sign, dey laughs and say good, and it make all
mine customers dink dat I cheat dem.'

" 'Is that all?' inquired a bystander.

" 'No,' said the German, emphatically, 'I can tell
you more as dat.'

" 'But how do you know these boys did all these
things,' inquired another.

" 'All de beeples say dey is de fellers,' was the
reply.

" 'What did they do to-night?' inquired another of
the crowd.

" 'Vell I tell you dat,' said the persecuted mer-
chant. 'To night I vas shtand in front von mine
shtore, to talk mit a carman, who have bring some
dings to me. Pretty soon, he get on his cart and
drive off, and ven he shtart, a parrell von botatoes,
dat shtand on de edge fon de shtep-valk, tip over in
de shtreet, and de botatoes fall out and shcatter
about, and the parrell it go yumping along de
shtreets, mit. de cart; I holler for de carman and he
shtop. Ven I go to see, I find dat a rope vas tie
round the parrel, and hitch to de cart-veel close; vell,

I bick up de botatoes, and put de parrel vonce more on de shtep-valk, and keep vatch. Soon I see dese boys come along, and dey look at me mit de tuyvel in deir eyes, and I know it vas dem. Yust den I run and ketch dem.'

"The details of the case being pretty well understood, it became a question with the crowd what should be done. The general opinion was that the boys were wrong in their continued annoyances of the Dutchman, though they did not think the case was one sufficiently aggravated to justify their being turned over either to the police or to the vengeance of the grocery-man. At last a portly old Knickerbocker, who had laughed heartily at the Dutchman's narration, essayed to act as spokesman.

"'What's your name,' said he to one of the boys with assumed gravity.

"'Mike Hannegan,' said he, 'and this 'ere boy is Barney Doolan.'

"'Oh, you young rascals,' continued the gentleman, 'you deserve to be arrested for your bad ways. You are very bad boys, you know you are, whether you are the ones who have bothered the Dutchman or not. He guessed right, I think, in supposing you to be the boys. But if these gentlemen will let you off, will you stop troubling him in the future ?'

8

" ' Yes, sir,' said both of the boys, meekly.

" ' Then cut stick, both of you,' said he.

" Just then an individual with a remarkable loafer-ish air, dressed in a blue single-breasted frock coat, with a row of military buttons, a blue cap with silver mountings, and a brass star on his breast—an individual, in brief, known as a policeman—arrived on the spot, and inquired what was the trouble. After informing him that he was a day after the fair, I left the vicinity."

When Mr. Van Dam concluded, on motion of Mr. Boggs it was

Resolved, that the members of the club do now proceed, each man for himself, to light his pipe.

The resolution was acceded to without a dissenting voter.

Dennis, Wagstaff, and Overdale, as usual, had been investigating in company, Overdale taking the lead, and Wagstaff taking notes, and all three occasionally taking egg-noggs.

A unanimous call was made for Wagstaff's note-book, which was immediately forthcoming.

The reading of Mr. Wagstaff's notes was prefaced by statements on the part of Dennis and Overdale which made the following facts apparent to the club. The previous evening the three went into a Green-

wich street bar-room, on the invitation of Overdale
to pay a visit to Delmonico's, to get a piece of pie
and some cigars. Whilst partaking of the order, a
singular person entered the room. His beauty was
decidedly of the yard-stick character. He was long
as a projected Iowa railroad, and as symmetrical as
a fence-rail; his face was as expressionless as the
head of Shakspeare which is seen on the drop-cur-
tain of the Broadway Theatre, surrounded by a
triple row of attenuated sausages. His square and
angular shoulders made him resemble a high-shoul-
dered pump, while his arms moved with as much ease
and grace as the handle to the same. Long, black
hair, parted in the middle, was soaped down until
the oleaginous ends reposed upon the unctuous collar
of his seedy coat. His shirt-collar, guiltless of starch,
was unbuttoned at the neck and laid far back over
his vest, doubtless to display a neck which, had it
been cut off, was long enough to tie.

He had seated himself, and had settled down into
a misanthropic quiet, when a little stubby man, with
one eye—the very ideal of a Washington market
butcher—happened to enter. As soon as the first-
mentioned subject saw him, he jumped up, rushed
at the stubby man, and had hardly touched him,
before a blow from the fist of the stubby man caused

him to collapse on the floor. The stubby man followed up his success by pulling the nose of his fallen
enemy, and threatening to give him a " tolerable
shake-up, if he ever came round his shop agin'."

The conflict was brief, as it soon drew in quite a
crowd, and amongst others a policeman. The tall
man was pointed out as the aggressor, but the stubby
man said " he didn't want to appear agin' the crack-
brained cuss ; that he guessed he (the said cuss) had
got the worst of it."

But the assembled multitudes were not satisfied.
They thought it was due to them that they should
have an explanation, and as the tall individual seemed
anxious, and the stubby individual didn't make any
objections, a ring was formed to give the parties a
chance to be heard.

The stubby man said that while the other was
" exercisin' his jaw, he'd have some ham'neggs ;"
whilst he was eating, the tall individual told his
story, which was one of blighted hopes, disappointed
expectations, unrequited love, and unappreciated
genius. Wagstaff's notes of his words read as follows :

" ' My name is Julius Jenkins, and I have a cousin
named Betsey Brown ; I love my cousin Betsey ;
have always loved my cousin Betsey, from the time
when as children we tore in loving partnership our

mutual pantalets and petticoats (for these legs once wore pantalets, and their symmetry was hidden from admiration by petticoats), looking for black-berries in a cedar-swamp ; from the time we sucked eggs together in the barn-yard and 'teetered' in happy sport upon the same board; from the time we built playhouses in the garden and made puppy-love behind the currant bushes; from those happy days of rural felicity until the present time, my cousin Betsey has been the ideal of my soul. We used to eat bread and milk out of the same bowl, dig angleworms with the same shovel, go fishing in the same creek, steal apples from the same orchard, and crawl through the same hole in the fence when the man chased us. Through all my lonely life the memory of cousin Betsey has been my guardian angel. I have been exposed to dire temptations ; once I was reduced to such extremity that I was about to earn my dinner by sawing wood, but my cousin Betsey seemed to rise before me and say, "Julius, don't degrade yourself;" and I didn't. I cast the saw to the earth, and begged my dinner from a colored washerwoman. I once accepted a situation as a clerk in a retail grocery. I stayed a week, but on every barrel of sugar, on every bar of soap, in every keg of lard, in each individual pota-to, in every bushel in all the cellar, I saw the reproachful face of my cousin Betsey; it rose before me from the oily depths of the butter-firkin, and from the cratery interior of the milk-can; the very peanuts rose up in judgment against me, and had on each separate end a speaking likeness of my cousin Betsey, which said, "Julius, don't degrade yourself;" I couldn't stand it; in the darkness of night I packed up my wardrobe (comprising one shirt of my own and two I borrowed from a neighboring clothes-line), helped myself to the small change, and vanished; I became a painter, I executed a portrait of my cousin Betsey; I asked a critical friend to see my master-piece; he gazed a moment, and then asked me which was the tail end; the dolt! he thought I meant it for a pig; I wrote poetry to my cousin Betsey, but the printer returned it because I spelled Cupid with a K, and put the capitals at the wrong end of my words; the uninformed ass; he did not understand the eccentricities of genius; I became an actor, and attempted Othello; at the rise of the curtain I was saluted with a shower of onions from appreciative friends, and at its fall I was presented by the manager with a brush, to which he added his gratuitous advice that I should keep the paint on my face and go into the boot-blacking business; I turned composer, but could never get my " Bootjack Waltz " published, or my oratorio of " The Ancient Applewoman" before the public; at last my cousin Betsey came to live in the city, and I thought once more to possess her love, but I found a rival; a one-eyed butcher; I wrote letters to her; I know that they should have been tied with blue ribbon, but necessity dictated cotton twine; I sent her presents; not so valuable as I could have wished; my intention was good but my means were limited; I could have wished to offer gold and jewels, but I could never afford more than a string of smelts, or half a pint of huckleberries; I resolved to serenade my cousin Betsey; I procured a violin, strung with the daintiest

filaments ever made from the bowels of the most delicate female feline infant; I repaired beneath her window and commenced my song, but the butcher came to the window, threw down a dime, and told me to go away; he took me for an organ-grinder; I indignantly stamped the money into the earth, but thought

again, picked it up and purchased some brandy to
nerve me for a desperate deed ; I had resolved to see
that butcher, to meet that butcher, to challenge that
butcher, to fight that butcher, to conquer that
butcher or to die ; yesterday I went to that butcher's
shop to execute my design, but he kicked me out·
To day I came in here in despair ; who should come
in but the butcher; now was my chance ; I rushed at
him, but my personal strength was not equal to the
task ; he boxed my ears, pulled my nose, and I was
cheated out of my revenge, simply because I wasn't
able to lick him.   Now I demand of this intelligent
assembly, as a matter of right, the instant annihila-
tion of the one-eyed butcher now present, the author
of all my miseries, that my Betsey may be restored
to me.'

"Mr. Jenkins sank into a chair, exhausted by his
effort.

"The butcher wiped his chops on a red silk handkerchief, and then proceeded to tell his story, which
was as follows, as appears by Wagstaff's notes ;

"'This here feller's allers botherin' my wife,
'cause he says she's his'n; yesterday he gits drunk,
comes in my place, and wants to fight me.   I told
him to leave, and he wouldn't, so I hussled him out.
I happened to come in here jus' now, and he comes

at me. I doubles him up, and that's the hull story.'

" The laconic statement of the one-eyed stubby butcher satisfied the parties assembled that Mr. Jenkins's insane pursuit of another man's wife had justly brought upon him the indignation of the husband, and he was advised very generally, in the future, to cease all importunities of a similar character.

" Finding that his story excited no sympathy in his behalf, Mr. Jenkins left the place in disgust, and the three Elephantines soon after left in an omnibus."

Mr. Spout here arose, and said he liked the story in all of its parts, except the concluding joke, which he considered to be, not only unkind, but uncalled for. He should take the liberty of considering it expunged from the records.

Some member here dared to suggest that it was high time that the Higholdboy should do something else than criticise the contributions of his fellow-members.

Mr. Spout desired it to be understood that he should admit of no dictation from inferiors; that he should exercise his own discretion in deciding whether he would contribute to the amusement of others, or criticise them in their efforts to be jolly. Yet, without giving up any of this right, he would volun-

8*

teer to lay before the club, on the present occasion, a matter which, to him, possessed some points of interest, and as he didn't care whether it interested the others or not, he should state facts for his own amusement.   He intended to laugh at everything which he thought was funny, without any reference to the comfort of others.

"The circumstance which I am about to relate," said Mr. Spout, "is one in which a friend of mine was involved.   My friend's name," he continued, "is Bartholomew Buxton.   He is the owner of a book-store, and was led into that business on account of a thirst for reading.   He is a man of about thirty-five years, and his whole life has been passed in poring over books.   I regard him as a man of very rare intelligence, though his intellect is not, perhaps, very fruitful of original thoughts.   What is remark-able with him is his personal appearance.   He is a little man, just large enough to be entitled to enter the army—that is to say, 'five-foot-four.'   His body is very small, and his head very large, round, and full.   His hair is of a sandy color, and of the scratch wig order of cut.   His eyes are small, and one of them squints frightfully.   His complexion is quite pale.   In the matter of dress, he wears usually a pair of pants of a checker-board-pattern on-a-large-

scale cloth, blue dress-coat, ornamented with large
fancy brass buttons, and a vest—a double-breaster—
of the brightest scarlet. But these eccentricities in
apparel would hardly attract attention so long as the
main feature of his dress is visible. That feature is
his collar. It is a remarkable collar—a mighty ram-
part of linen, which encircles his head in a line
with the centres of his ears, almost meeting in his
face. Numerous reasons have been assigned for Mr.
Buxton's going to such lengths (or rather heights)
in his indulgence in collar. One idea advanced is,
that he is actuated by a desire to economize in the
expenses of washing, and to do this, has the garments made in such a way as to be convertible into
collars at either end. Another suggestion is, that
the collar is a matter of utility, designed by Mr.
Buxton to economize physical strength, which, inasmuch as his head is very large and his body very
small, must be overtaxed to hold his ponderous
brain-box erect.

"Gentlemen, three days since I received a call
from my friend Buxton. He appeared melancholy
and dejected, which surprised me; but what surprised me more, in respect to his present appearance,
was the manifest disarrangement of his collar. It
did not stand up on one side with the majestic erect-

ness which characterized it on the other. On the left it was hanging down flabbily; its self-sustaining power was departed.

"I saw, by his countenance, that something important to him had occurred, and the appearance of his collar only tended to confirm my suspicions. I accordingly asked him what was the trouble.

" 'Trouble,' said he, 'enough of it. Sir,' he continued, 'last night I was locked up in a cell at the station-house, for exercising the privileges of a free-man—a native American citizen. I was arrested, and violently dragged off to that cell, where I remained last night, and this morning was tried before the magistrate, only, however, to be acquitted. What made it worse was, that I should be arrested with a nigger, and be tried with a nigger, and acquitted with a nigger. He was a huge nigger—a colossal nigger—a nigger fully six feet and four inches in height; his face betrayed no evidence of light—it was all shade; he was a nigger, above all others, so black, that he would make an excellent drum-major to a funeral procession, if custom sanctioned the employment of that non-commissioned official on such occasions. Inasmuch, however, as custom doesn't do any such thing, the next best use to which the sable giant could be put, would be to make his face the figurehead of a Broadway mourning store; with the exception of his large size and remarkable black face, the nigger in question looked very much like other niggers not in question. He was a nigger, in fact, who gave as his name the half-classic and half-descriptive appellation of Cesar Freeman. I have always been a "woolly-head" until now, but may I be bursted if I don't go and join the Know Nothings to-morrow, and begin a crusade against all niggers—particularly nigger-giants and nigger women.

"'How did this occur?' I inquired, anxiously.

"'I'll tell you,' said he. 'But before doing so however, I desire to state a fact. We have all our human weaknesses; indeed, it may be set down as a truism that human beings do have human weaknesses to a greater or less extent; I am a human being; I have my human weakness, and that weakness is my collars; it required years of experiment to bring my collars to their present perfection; nearly all of the quarrels I ever had have been with laundresses who have failed to do them up to my liking; if a man wishes to ruffle my temper he need only to ruffle my collar, and it is accomplished; tell me the Savings Bank, where I deposit my extra money, has collapsed in the region of the money-vault; tell me that I have

got to attend a charity ball; give me the jumping
toothache; place me in a Bowery stage with fourteen
inside, and I in juxtaposition to a dirty woman with
a squalling baby who has got the seven years' itch—
all of these I can bear, but when it comes to interfere with my collars it is going a point too far. Now
I come to the time when unforeseen circumstances
brought me in violent collision with this nigger of
African extraction; I was walking down the street,
near where the belligerent demonstration took place,
when I saw directly in front of me a long-tailed man in
an amiable-appearing coat—no—an amiable-appearing coat in a long-tailed—no—I mean an amiable
appearing man in a long-tailed coat. For my life I
could not conceive why that amiable individual's
proclivities in matters of apparel should lead him to
wear a garment of so ridiculous a cut. I had just
come to the sage conclusion that it was because
every donkey in the country chooses to have his hips
appear high or low to suit the caprice of Broadway
tailors, when at that moment the amiable person,
together with his long-tailed coat, was driven from
my mind. I became suddenly conscious that an important event had transpired. An elderly female nigger, in throwing water on a store-window which she
was cleaning, did not confine her professional favors

exclusively to the window for which she had been
hired, but she disbursed copious supplies of Croton
upon the passers-by, for which she had not been
hired. In fact, I am bold to assert, that several
persons were favored with several gratuitous duck-
ings by this colored female. I was one of those
persons; a bountiful current of water interrupted
the current of my thoughts; like a juvenile Nia-
gara, it dashed against my collar in the left side,
as you can see. Now, my collar is impervious to
perspiration, but it could not stand up under the
soaking of a cataract; as my collar fell my choler
rose ; I looked around at the sable author of my
troubles, and I saw on her face an exultant grin at
what she had done. I felt as if I would like to have
crammed a wet broom which she had in her hand
down her throat, splint end downwards; for obvious
reasons I did not do this; but I did speak to her in
language expressive of my emphatic disapprobation
of the unasked-for and informal baptism with which
she had been pleased to favor me; I suppose my
words must have frightened her; at any rate she
fell off from a stool on which she was elevated ; she
gave a scream ; this black Hercules came down the
stairs ; she informed him that I had insulted her ; he
looked at me with his teeth grinning as if he would

like to have eaten me without gravy or condiment; he gave one diabolical grin, and then came at me. I am not pugnacious; a lamb-like inoffensiveness has ever been my prominent characteristic; I have a constitutional repugnance to a fight, either with weapons natural or artificial; if loaded fire-arms are around I never feel so safe as when I see the butt-ends pointed at my vital parts; though not a member of the Peace Society, yet that society has ever had in me an ardent sympathizer; peaceful though I be, yet, when the sleeping lion within me is aroused, I know no bounds to my rage, and I insist upon going about, seeking whom I may devour; I saw the belligerent attitude of my enemy; he struck me; we grappled; an insatiable desire to taste the flesh of a colored man at that instant seized upon me; in a moment the digits of his right hand were between my teeth; I know that for a moment or two hostilities were active; I became conscious, too, that hostilities ceased; I soon learned the cause; the cause was the arrival of two policemen, who are always around when they shouldn't be, and never when they should. I was brought to the station-house.'

" 'Well, what took place before the court?' I asked.

" 'At seven this morning,' said Buxton, 'we were brought before the judge, and put in a pen; on one side of me was the aforesaid nigger, and on the other side a disgusting piece of feminine humanity; an importation from Ireland, who had just come off from a bender. Our names were finally called, the nigger's first, by all that's holy. Two officers who arrested us were the witnesses; they testified that on last evening, about dusk, they were engaged in conversation on the corner of a street which forms the boundary line between their respective beats, when they saw a crowd collected on the sidewalk, about a square above; they ran there, and they saw me and the nigger engaged in a fight; they said that the nigger was striking me violently with his left fist; his right hand was between my teeth, while I was kicking and striking the nigger very generally and promiscuously, and a nigger woman who was present was laying the blows on me with a broom whenever she could; at that moment they arrested me and the nigger; it required all their strength to secure us, such was the violence of our efforts to get away; hence they were unable to take the woman into custody.

" 'The judge showed the cussed bad taste to ask the nigger to make his statement first. The nigger said that I had insulted his wife, and had made improper proposals to her; that made me wrathy; I

told him that he was guilty of uttering a falsehood
before the court; emphatically pronounced his asser-
tion relative to my making an insulting proposal to
that feminine lump of animated charcoal, with whom
he very properly cohabited, to be an unequivocal lie;
I am no controversalist, and still less would I descend
from my exalted height to engage in a controversy
with that herculean African, especially after enduring the perspiration, which, despite my frantic
efforts to the contrary, I was compelled to suffer
during a hot night, in a cell where any respectable
thermometer, if it could be induced to go into the
cell once, if it was anything at all, would be a
hundred at least; yes, sir,' he continued, 'and should
you ever have a morbid desire to enter into controversy, recline your heated form of a hot night in the
cell which I occupied, and by morning you will
insist upon retiring into some secluded spot, from
which secluded spot you can look dispassionately and
unmoved upon the moral strifes of the world.

" 'Well, the up-shot of the matter was that both
of us were discharged.'

" I gave Mr. Buxton what consolation I could,
after which he took his departure to put on a new
collar."

When Mr. Spout had concluded his narration, he

proceeded to awaken such of the members of the club as were still present, telling them that it was time to go home. But he did not succeed in fully arousing them to an appreciation of the lateness of the hour, until he had put ice into their boot-legs and shirt-bosoms.

The Club in an Uproar.

How doth the little busy bee
Improve each shining hour
And gather honey all the day
From every opening——

Towards
nine o'clock one
evening, the members of the club had casually con-
vened in the club-room, although no notice had been
given that they were to assemble on that occasion.
The only absentee was Johnny Cake, but this created
no surprise, as the wonder was, not why any member
was absent, but why so many were present.

An hour was passed in discussing the current
events of the day, when some member suggested,
that if anybody had anything to offer, either amusing
or instructive, an excellent opportunity was now
afforded.

It so happened that Mr. Remington Dropper had

138

in his pocket a quantity of foolscap, on which he had written a statement of certain experience, with which he had been favored on the previous day.

A general wish was expressed that Mr. Dropper might make himself useful in the exigency. He consented, and after the members had lighted their pipes, the barkeeper had been signalized for eight whisky-punches, and the Higholdboy had seated himself in his chair, the meeting was declared to be duly organized.

Mr. Dropper commenced:

"Yesterday," said he, "I had the pleasure of see-ing our favorite quadruped as he appeared on Broadway, from an omnibus, whilst on a voyage from the South Ferry to Union Square. At half-past two o'clock I went over the ferry to Hamilton Avenue, Brooklyn. Having transacted my business, set out on my return, jumped aboard the ferry-boat and was soon on the New York side ; stepped outside the gate, when I was beset by two dozen different omnibus agents, and as many different drivers. ' Here y'ar, right up Broadway.' ' Wide awake, 'ere Bower' un' Gran' street.' ' Right up Broadway, Sixth Avenue.' ' Here's Broad'ay, Bleeck' street, un' Eigh thavenue.' ' Here y'ar Bowery un' Ouston street.'

"'I want to go to Greenwich Avenue,' said a timid old gentleman.

"'Here y'ar,' said the agent, as he took the old gentleman by the seat of his pantaloons, and threw him head first into an East Broadway stage.

"The old gentleman, as soon as he could recover from his astonishment, looked out of the window at the agent.

"'Sir,' said he, 'does this stage carry me to Greenwich Avenue?'

"'Certing,' was the prompt reply, "you'll get there, never fear. Here's Eas' Broadway un' Dry Dock.'

"'Where do you want to go madam?' asked the Ninth Avenue stage-agent of a lady accompanied by a little boy.

"'To the Crystal Palace,' said the lady.

"'Here y'ar then,' said he, as he placed her in the stage which probably stopped fully three quarters of a mile from the place.

"At last, all the persons desiring to ride had secured seats in stages, but whether *the* stages they desired is quite doubtful. I jumped in a Broadway and Fourteenth street stage, the agent gave the door two slams, and off we started. The passengers were an old maid with a poodle dog, a young miss who had just put on a long dress, a German, an old buffer who occupied space for two, and myself. Suddenly we stopped in Whitehall street, on our larboard side we find ourselves caught against a Sixth Avenue stage coming down, and our starboard quarter caught against the hubs of a cart. Carman apologetic— Sixth Avenue stage-driver affable. Passengers frightened. Maiden lady with poodle dog exclaimed, ' Oh, dear me !' Poodle dog barked. Fat gentle· man thought that stage-drivers now-a-days were growing too careless. Got under way. Sighted Bowling Green off our port bow. Female from Ireland with native infant hailed the vehicle. Driver stopped. Female from Ireland tumbled up the steps. Driver slammed the door, which struck the female from Ireland a severe blow in the rear. Result, female from Ireland lying prostrate on the floor, and native infant lying around loose on the person of the old maid, in the particular premises claimed by the poodle dog. Poodle dog barked and snapped at native infant ; native infant cried. Old maid scolds female from Ireland. Female from Ireland takes up native infant, and anathematizes poodle dog. Fat gentleman suggests that it's all the result of the recklessness of the driver. Old lady and female from Ireland pacified. German female, with

a basket of dirty clothes, seeks admittance. Driver
accommodating.   Enter German female, and exit
myself.   Take my position on top with the driver.
Band of music heard in the direction of Wall street.
Target company turn into Broadway.   Inebriated
negro carrying a target, on which is inscribed,
'Michael Flinn Guard, Capt. Pat. Sweeny.'   Horse
attached to a buggy coming down Broadway, unused
to military demonstrations—unaccustomed to the
noises of sixteen German gentlemen, making frantic
efforts to blow their brains out through brass horns.
Horse rears and plunges into the rank and file of the
Michael Flinn Guard.   Consternation of the infantry
at an unexpected attack from the cavalry.   Cavalry
triumphant.   Michael Flinn Guard commence throwing stones at individual in the buggy.   Individual
drives off.   Plethoric German scrapes himself up,
and finds the starch entirely taken out of his ophi-
cleide.   German with light moustache has lost the
mouth-piece of his E flat saxe horn ; Michael Flinn
Guards endeavoring to find their arms.   Irish corporal unable to discover his bayonet.   First lieutenant
finds his sword run through the tenor drum.
Ambitious private finds the pewter cake-basket he
won as a prize, with the butt end of a musket through
it.   Guns in several instances in fragments ; swords

broken; brass horns disjointed, and, as a consequence, music *non est.* By general consent, Michael
Flinn Guards break ranks and disperse. Lady with
hoop skirts hails the driver. Driver again obliging.
Enter hoop skirts. Gentleman with a baby-wagon
hails driver. 'Whoa-'p.' Astonishing driver. Gentleman lifts up the baby-wagon on the top. Driver
receives it, and gently smashes it in pieces. Gentleman gets inside. Dropsical individual on the starboard quarter hails us. The gentleman enters, and
again we are under way. Teutonic target company
turn into Broadway from Courtlandt street—'The
Lager Bier Invincibles, Capt Conrad Künzmüller.'
Suddenly find ourselves smashed up amid a perfect
labyrinth of carts, stages, buggies, wagons, horses,
mules, cotton bales, boxes, furniture, drivers,
policemen, passengers, pedestrians, &c. A wagon-
load of dirt on our port side—wagon-driver unso-
phisticated; unused to driving in New York. In
advance a cart having two bales of hay on board.
Our horses, having nothing else to do, make efforts
to get at the hay. Our driver again accommodating.
He gets down and unchecks the horses. Horses proceed to make inroads upon property not belonging to
the omnibus company. Carman discovers the larceny. Indignant carman. Hits our horses ov   the

head with the butt end of his whip. Reciprocal indignation. Our driver gives carman a cut across his proboscis with a long lash.

" Our progress continues.

" Fat gentleman impatient. Reasserts his previously-expressed conviction, that the stage is an imposition : says he'll get out. Driver insists on payment. Fat gentleman passes up a quarter. Driver passes him back a ten-cent piece and eight cents. Fat gentleman insists that he is swindled to the extent of one cent, which he demands. Driver very obliging, and 'don't he wish he may get it." Fat gentleman gets out, but finds himself  completely surrounded by vehicles, and without a possibility of being able to reach the curbstone in safety, concludes to enter the stage again. Driver refuses to open the door. Fat gentleman demands to be admittted. Driver says he'll see him blowed first. Fat gentleman frantic, but driver incorrigible. At last fat gentleman gets on his hands and knees, and, after crawling under a team of horses and the tails of two carts, reaches the sidewalk. Again moving. Irish female with native infant pulls the strap. Driver accommodating. Female inquires if this is a Bowery stage. Driver says no. Female insists upon getting out. Driver insists, with equal warmth, that, as a prior condition, she must disgorge a sixpence. Female indisposed to comply. Old maid with the poodle dog gives the strap three convulsive jerks. 'Whoa-'p.' Old maid says that native infant, belonging to female from Ireland, has the ship fever. Female from Ireland indignantly denies the statement, and says that it is *only* the itch. Old maid swoons. Poodle dog barks at all the passengers generally, and the female from Ireland particularly. Dropsical gentleman puts some smelling-salts under the nose of old maid. Happy result. Old maid revives, and asks if anybody beside herself was injured by the explosion. Sight Fulton street off our starboard bow. Enter Fifth Avenue and Amity street stages, R. 1st Entrance. Exit Irish porter with a load of band-boxes, L. 1st Entrance, in time to save his bacon and band-boxes. New feature coming up Fulton street from the East River— 'The Sour Krout Guards, Captain Wilhelm Stein,' in return from target excursion. Still another feature coming up Fulton street from North River— 'The Patrick Gaffney Grenadiers, Captain Timothy

Leahey,' on a return from target excursion.   Two
companies approach one another.   Menacing looks on
the part of the Sour Krout Guards.   Bellicose attitude of the Gaffney Grenadiers.   Belligerent mani-
festation of the Sour Krouts; corporal of the Gaffneys throws a brick at the Sour Krouts.   Sour
Krouts boiling over with indignation, make a demonstration.   Both companies unused to the man-
agement of firelocks, but accustomed to war and
carnage.   They lay down their arms and take up
their fists.   General, promiscuous, and miscellaneous
shoulder-hitting by the strength of both companies.
Enter third party.   Mad bull rushes down Broadway
and pitches into the hottest of the fight, with horns
down and tail up.   Sour Krouts and Gaffneys in
consternation fly from the scene of the struggle in
all directions.   Mad bull makes a descent into a
mock auction shop.   Stool pigeons and auctioneer
all knocked down without a bidder.   Sudden fall in
pinchbeck watches.   Bull stands for a moment in a
contemplative mood over the devastation, and then
walks away with a dignified air.   Barnum's in sight.
Lady and three children get inside.   Female from
Ireland with native infant concludes to pay the sixpence and get out.   Astor House in the usual place.
Barclay street in the distance.   By way of variety,

a company turn into Broadway, 'The Tugmutton Terribles, Captain Frightful Buster,' in a return from a target excursion at Hoboken. The captain elevated, lieutenants inebriated, privates intoxicated, the nigger target-bearer drunk — effect of having eaten too many ham sandwiches. Stage again immobile. Two Hoosiers get inside, and ask the driver to stop at the St. Nicholas Tavern. Funeral procession coming down Broadway. Forty-nine carriages. Learned that the remains of Dennis Hooligan, the keeper of a corner grocery in Hammersley street, were being conveyed to their last resting-place. Just as the hearse reaches Anthony street a ponderous cart crosses Broadway. Wheels fifteen feet in diameter. Steamboat boiler suspended under the axletree. Majestic vehicle fetches up all standing against a cart loaded with flour. Fall in breadstuffs. Prodigal distribution of flour. Hearse and funeral procession in close proximity.

" Vehicles accumulate. Great commotion among drivers. Procession mixed up in an indiscriminate verbal war. At last hearse manages to go down towards the Five Points. The procession succeeds in getting out by turning in the other direction, except the rear portion, which, to my knowledge, never got out. Once more under way, and making

good time.   Man with a gold-headed cane stops the
stage, and passes up a five-cent piece.   Driver
swears, and advises him to ride in the cars hereafter.
Driver suggests that he is full ten minutes behind
time, and is bound to make it up.   Lays on the lash,
much to the surprise of the animals.   Driver pulls
up in front of the St. Nicholas Hotel, and announces
the spot through the money-hole.   Nobody essays to
pass up any fare.   Driver repeats the announcement.
Nobody moves.   Driver inquires, impatiently, if
there ain't ' two fellers inside wot wanted to git out at
the St. Nicholas Hotel.'   Still no reply.   Again the
inquiry.   One of the Hoosiers said he asked him to
' stop at the St. Nicholas tarvern, 'cause why, 'cause
he wanted to see it.   He'd seen it enough ; it was a
purty nice tarvern, he reckoned, and he might drive
on.'   Driver gave the horses an extra cut, and we
move again.   Asthmatic party pulls the strap.
After feeling in all of his pockets for two minutes,
informs the driver that he left his *porte-monnaie* in
his other pantaloons.   Driver says the story won't go
down—that the game is too old.   Party tries to make
his exit, but the door won't open, the driver holding
hard on the strap.   Asthmatic party threatens to
horsewhip driver.   Driver says, ' any time when
conwenyent he hoped he'll make the trial.'   Driver

about to start, when asthmatic party pulls out his jack-knife and cuts the strap. Asthmatic party triumphs. Driver, frantic with rage, throws an apple at asthmatic party, and hits asthmatic party on his knowledge-box. Asthmatic party falls, and upsets an apple-stand. Celtic female, the proprietor of the apple-stand, hits asthmatic party with a brick. Both parties close in, and fight amid the ruins of the apple-stand. Driver starts the horses, but looks around to watch the fight. Horses sheer off to the starboard, and the hub of the hind wheel breaks down a lamp-post. Driver observes policeman approaching at a rapid speed. No time to survey the ruins, so he applies the lash, and we move away from the scene of the mishap at a speed ominous of swift destruction to horse-shoes and wagon-tires. Female, with three children, calls out to stop, and passes up a three-dollar bill. Driver inquires if she hasn't got any change. Female gives a negative response. Driver gives change in small pieces, retaining as fare the moderate sum of seventy-five cents for a woman and three children. Woman attempts to count the change. Driver sings out to 'Hurry up — behind time — can't wait all day.' Female bewildered, leaves with her children, and driver whips up the horses, remarking that he

'guesses she'll learn, after a while, not to pass up
bills for stage-fare.' Soon reach Union Square.
Tell the driver I'll get off. Offer him a sixpence.
Driver says, 'he'll not take a cent; that if there ever
was a nout-'n'-outer, I'm one, and he hopes that it
won't be the last time we'll meet; and if he only
had time, he wouldn't let me off without treatin'
me.' I thanked him for his good opinion, shook
hands, and jumped off the box.

"Thus, gentlemen," concluded Mr. Dropper,
"ends the history of my voyage on an omnibus."

Mr. Quackenbush arose, and stated that he
regarded Mr. Dropper's paper as a valuable addition
to the historical writings of the country. He therefore moved that a gold medal be prepared by a committee of the club, of which the Higholdboy should
not be an *ex-officio* member, for presentation to Mr.
Dropper. Mr. Dropper to pay the whole expense
of procuring the same, and to stand a champagne
supper for the honor conferred on him.

The motion was carried with only one dissenting
voice—that of Mr. Dropper, who said he didn't want
any such expensive and equivocal honors.

The presiding officer informed Mr. Dropper that
he was fined three cents for contempt of club.

Over an hour was now passed in a state of inac-

tivity. Some of the members slept and some didn't.
As a means of inducing excitement of some kind, a
member signalized the institution on the first floor
for pork and beans for the entire crowd. This was
promptly answered, and for a time the club had
enough to engage its attention. After the aforesaid
luxuries had been duly disposed of, the members
proceeded to take seats, lie on the floor, prop themselves against the wall, and hang themselves up on a
peg, as best suited their independent fancies. The
presiding officer announced that the rules on this
occasion would be enforced strictly Accordingly,
each individual present began to do exactly what
pleased him, without any regard to the comfort,
convenience, or personal predilections of anybody
else. The Higholdboy first secured the left boot of
every member present. After pulling a boot on each

leg of the table, he put
one on each of his hands,
like a gauntlet, and then
laid the seventh on the
table. The object of Mr.
Spout, in pursuing this
eccentric course of conduct, soon became apparent,
when he laid himself on the table, using the aforesaid solitary boot as a pillow, it being manifest that
9*

he desired to preclude the possibility of an adjourn-ment during the nap, and inasmuch as it would be found inconvenient for the members to leave the premises with but a single pedal covering, and as it would be impossible for a member to secure the other, without awakening the most venerable and exceedingly somnolent Higholdboy, it will be appa-rent to the credulous reader that Mr. Spout's idea was quite ingenious.

Under these circumstances, each member deter-mined to make himself as comfortable as the time, the place, and the conveniences would admit of.

Mr. Boggs was lying flat on his back, trying to drink a hot whisky-punch without breaking the tumbler, spilling the liquor, or getting the sugar inside his whiskers. Mr. Overdale was learning "juggling without a master," and was endeavoring to spin plates on his whalebone cane. In striving to acquire this elegant accomplishment, he had broken all the dishes in the premises. As he varied his plate-spinning endeavors with repeated trials at tossing the cups and balls, for which purpose he used the tumblers and coffee-cups, and as, whenever he caught one cup, he dropped two, and stepped on the fragments, the work of demolition went bravely on.

Mr. Van Dam amused himself by blacking the faces of all the pictures in the room with charcoal. Dennis employed himself for an hour and a half in whittling off with a jack-knife one leg of every chair in the apartment, so as to make it four inches shorter than the rest. Wagstaff collected all the books he could find, and piled them into a shaky pyramid, which he was preparing to push over with a broomstick upon the head of the unconscious High-oldboy.

Quackenbush had not been idle; taking advantage of the drowsiness of his superior officer, he had sewed the bottoms of that gentleman's pantaloons together with a waxed end, after which he made a moustache on himself with burned cork, and then painted the left side of his face in three-cornered patches like a sleepy harlequin, dyed his shirt-collar scarlet with red ink, and went to sleep in the corner to await the result, having first tripped up Mr. Over-dale, who, by way of a new variation in his juggling performances, was now trying to balance the poker on his nose, while he held a rocking-chair in one hand and a hat-box full of oyster shells in the other. Dropper had a checker-board before him, and was superintending a game between his right and left hand.

But suddenly, those of the Elephants who were in their waking senses, became sensible of a noise outside. It begun at the foot of the stairs, like the sound of a regiment of crazy Boston watchmen, all springing their rattles at once. The noise became louder, and seemed to be coming up the stairs, and now rivalled in sound a mail-train on a race. Now the uproar became more distinct, and evidently proceeded from some person or persons outside, who were provided with some ingenious facilities for kicking up a row, with which ordinary roisterers are unacquainted. These persons now began a furious attack upon the "outer walls." Mr. Overdale paused in his plate-breaking occupation, long enough to pour out a few emphatic sentences, addressed to the individuals outside, in which he consigned them to a locality too hot for a powder-mill, and then resumed his practice.

As the door began to shake, Overdale laid down the poker, smashed what few large pieces of plates were left over the head of the recumbent Quackenbush, awoke the Higholdboy by rolling him off the table, aroused the rest of the party by a few kicks in the ribs, and then, undoing the fastenings of the door, was proceeding to expostulate with the disturbers. No sooner, however, had he opened the

door, than a rush was made by the invaders, and
Mr. Dropper upset by the besieging party. Mr.
Dropper fell upon the stomach of the half-awakened
Quackenbush, they both pitched into Mr. Boggs, and
then all three rolled over the Higholdboy. This last-
named personage, having the bottoms of his pantaloons sewed together, could not arise until the
friendly jack-knife unfettered his lengthy legs. All
parties being restored to the perpendicular, an immediate inquiry was made into the cause of the disturbance.

Then it was discovered that the person who had
kicked up this diabolical bobbery was no less a personage than the heretofore discreet and temperate
Johnny Cake, aided and abetted by an individual
unknown to the rest of the company, but whose
appearance bespoke him to be one of the boys, who,
although not an "Elephant," presented at first
sight distinguished claims to be honored with that
enviable distinction.

Yes, Johnny Cake, the man who would never be
persuaded to taste a glass of liquor of any kind,
who had always endeavored to keep his companions
from spirituous imbibition; the virtuous cold-water-
ite, whom the sight of a glass of brandy would give
a cold chill, a whisky-punch throw into spasms, or a

mug of "lager" give a teetotal convulsion, stood
now before the astounded Elephantine brotherhood
drunk, plainly, undeniably, unequivocally *drunk*.

He had a black eye, and a swelled nose. His coat
was on hind side before, and buttoned between his
shoulders, while his pantaloons were entirely bereft
of buttons, and were secured from parting company
only by two pieces of telegraph-wire which, with
commendable ingenuity, he had converted into
extemporaneous metallic suspenders. His companion was in a singular state of derangement as to his
personal attire, having no coat at all, and a red shirt
over his nether continuations.

As soon as the first expression of surprise was
over, the Higholdboy, comprehending that something unusual had taken place, ordered the company
to be seated. In obedience to this peremptory order
from the most noble officer of the club, the Elephantines each took a seat, but as the inglorious young
man before-mentioned had made the chairs exceedingly treacherous and insecure, by cutting off one
.leg of each, the immediate consequence of the
attempt was another general sprawlification upon the
floor, executed in a masterly manner by the entire
strength of the company. After five minutes of vigorous polyglot profanity had somewhat relieved the

feelings of the fallen Elephantines, and they had recovered their feet, they contrived to sit down ; the chairs were as treacherous as ever, but being forewarned, the members were forearmed, and by dint of many exertions, contrived to maintain their seats with a tolerable show of dignity.

Johnny Cake was too far gone to make any intelligible replies, or give any account of himself, and it was resolved to postpone his examination until he should get sober. His companion, however, who seemed to be something in the theatrical way, gave his own story in his own peculiar manner, but refused to enlighten the anxious brotherhood about poor Johnny.

He possessed a facility of quotation equal to Richard Swiveller, Esq.'s, but he was as reckless about the exactitude of his extracts, and jumbled up his authorities with as much confusion as Captain Cuttle himself. He seldom gave a quotation right, but would break off in the middle and substitute some words of his own, or dovetail an irrelevant piece from some strange author, or mix up half-a dozen authors with interpolations of his own, in an inextricable verbal jumble.

The Higholdboy and the stranger held the following conversation :

" What's your name ?"

" Peter Knight; am a native to the marrow-bone. —That's Shakspeare."

" Young man, strange young man, young man to me unknown ; young man of the peculiar hat and ruby shirt, I fear to adapt my conversation to your evident situation ; that you're drunk, emphatically drunk, I repeat it, drunk—drunk was my remark— D—Runk, drunk."

" It's true, 'tis pity ; pity 'tis there isn't the devil a doubt of it.—That's Scott."

" Where did you get your liquor ?"

" Where the bee sucks, there sucks Peter Knight all day. Thou base, inglorious slave, think'st thou I will reveal the noble name of him who gave me wine ? No, sir-ee, Bob.—That's Beaumont and Fletcher."

" Ante up or leave the board; that is to say fire away, let us know, we won't tell. Although we never drink, we like to know where drink we might get, in case of cholera, or colic."

" I do remember an apothecary and here-abouts he dwells ; no he don't, he lives over in the Bowery —but in his needy shop a codfish hangs, and on his shelves a beggarly account of empty bottles ; noting this penury to myself, I said, if any man did need a brandy-punch, whose sale is fifty dollars fine in

Gotham, here lives a caitiff wretch who has probably
got plenty of it under the counter.   Why should I
here conceal my fault?   Wine ho! I cried.   The
call was answered.   I have no wine, said he, but
plenty of whis—.   Silence! thou pernicious caitiff,
quoth I; thou invisible spirit of wine, since we can
get thee by no other name, why let us call thee gin
and sugar.   He brought the juice of cursed juniper
in a phial, and in the porches of my throat did pour
Udolpho Wolfe's distilment.   Thus was I by a
Dutchman's hand at once dispatched—not drunk or
sober—sent into the dirty streets three-quarters tight,
with all my imperfections on my head.   The fellow's
name? My very soul rebels.   But whether it is
nobler in the mind to suffer the cuffs and bruises
of this bloody Dutchman or to take arms against his
red-haired highness, and by informing end him?   I
go and it is done.   Villain, here's at thy heart!   His
name, your Honor, is Bobblesnoffkin in the Bowery.
That's Shakspeare mixed."

"Young man, whose shirt has escaped from all
control, and now hangs loose, the posterior section of
which has also sustained a serious, and, I fear, irre-
mediable fracture, I have another question to pro-
pound; answer upon your life.   Have you got a
home?"

" My home is on the deep, deep sea.—That's
Plutarch's Lives."

" How do you get your living ?"

" Doubt thou the stars are fire ; doubt that the sun
doth move ; doubt truth to be a liar, but never
doubt that I'll get a living while the oyster-sloops
don't have but one watchman.—That's Billy S.
again."

" Do you pay for your oysters ?"

" Base is the slave that pays ; the speed of thought
is in my limbs.—That's Byron."

" Do you steal them and then run away ?"

" I've told thee all, I'll tell no more, though short
the story be ; let me go back where I was before and
I'll get my living without troubling the corporation.
That's Tom Moore, altered to suit circumstances."

" You ought to dispense with the brandy and
gin."

" Oh, I could be happy with either, were 'tother
dear charmer bottled up and the cork put in.—That's
Dibdin with a vengeance."

" Young man, I fear you've led our young friend,
whom you now see asleep amongst the broken
crockery, from the paths of sobriety. What do you
suppose will become of you if you go on in this
way ?"

"Alas, poor Yorick!—Peter, I mean. Who knows where he will lay his bones? Few and short will the prayers be said, and nobody 'll feel any sorrow : but they'll cram him into his clay-cold bed, and bury somebody else on the top of him to-morrow; the minister will come, put on his robe and read the service; the choir 'll sing a hymn; earth to earth and dust to gravel, and that 'll be the last of Peter Knight."

The Higholdboy consulting with those members of the club who were still awake, it was resolved forthwith to put Peter Knight down stairs. As he went he remarked :

"Fare thee well, and if for ever, all the better.—That's Byron, revised and corrected."

Johnny Cake was manifestly too far gone to think of taking him to a hotel to sleep, and under these circumstances the club resolved itself into a committee of the whole, to remain in sleepy session all night, to take care of their prostrate fellow-member, Mr. Johnny Cake.

Johnny Cake's first Spree.

Whatever is, is.

WRIGHT.

In the last chapter of this veritable history is related the unexpected and unusually thorough inebriation of Mr. John I. Cake, from the verdant prairies of Illinois. The alcoholically-saturated condition of Johnny's corporosity, on the occasion herein-before-mentioned, surprised the thirsty brotherhood far more than would a similar state of facts in which any other one of the fraternity should have been implicated, because as Johnny had always perched himself upon the aqueous pinnacle of misanthropic teetotalism, it was not reasonable to suppose that he should, by one single dive, precipitate himself at once to the lowest depth of inebriation—for his profession's sake, he should have come down easier.

As his new-made friends had taken his moral culture under their especial guardianship, he was duly required, the next evening, to give, for the instruction and edification of the club, a full account of his night's experience.

Having first premised that he only complied with this desire in obedience to that imperative rule of the club, to which he had solemnly affixed his name, which, in the most awful language, pledges every member who takes that terrible obligation to do exactly as he pleases, unless his own pleasure shall influence him otherwise, or unless, upon mature consideration, he shall decide that he had rather do something else, he proceeded to enlighten the anxious Elephantine expectants.

"When I left you yesterday," said he, "I had no more idea that I should so far overstep the bounds of my customary propriety, and make my next

appearance before you in a state of alcoholic disguise, than I have at this present moment that the
setting sun will see me under arrest for picking
somebody's pocket of a steam saw-mill.   Strolling
about yesterday for some time, I became tired of the
monotonous hurry of Broadway, and eventually
strayed into that delightful rural locality which you
call, I think, the Bowery.

"On the corner of this avenue of the rustic cogno-
men and Broome street, there is a place of refresh-
ment for the weary.   I entered its open doors, and
sat down in a little three-sided closet, determined to
procure the wherewithal to refresh the inner individual.   Obedient to my upraised finger, a person
came.   This person had on a small white apron;
this person also flourished in his dexter-digits a napkin of questionable purity; this person wore slippers, and had a voice like an asthmatic bull-frog;
this person was a city waiter—a male waiter—a
degeneration of the genus homo, which I sincerely
hope will, at no very distant day, become utterly
extinct.   He procured for me the viands which my
capricious taste selected from the suggestive printed
list of edibles there to be obtained.   While engaged
in consigning to a living grave the bivalves he had
brought, I had a fair opportunity to observe some, to

me, remarkable gymnastics then in course of accomplishment by an active young man who presided at the bar, and held dominion over the bottles. First pouring into a tumbler some liquid, to me unknown, diluting it with water, adding ice, sugar, lemon, and other ingredients with which I am unacquainted, he proceeded to throw the compound about in the most unheard-of manner, from one tumbler to another, over his head, under his leg, round his neck, over one arm and under the other, without ever spilling a drop. First uplifting one hand high in air, he poured the mixture in a sparkling cascade from the glass in the right hand, to that in the left; then he threw it in a sparkling shower in the air, till the lumps of ice rattled on the ceiling; then he dispersed it in a misty spray about his head and recovered it all in his magic glass, by some diabolic dexterity, without losing the fraction of a drop; then, in one grand, final effort, he tossed it round the beer-pump, down one side, and up the other, and over the chandelier, changing a two-dollar bill while it was in the air, and giving his customer his drink with one hand, and with the other his silver change, intermixed with twenty per cent. of pewter dimes, which the thirsty buyer invariably pocketed before he could recover from his astonishment.

" I finished my dinner, and was anxious to see the
little man perform again. I approached the little
man, and desired him to concoct me a lemonade.
He inquired if I wanted a 'fly' in it. As the flying
part was what I most desired, I answered yes. The
little man went through the motions. I sent the
lemonade to its destination, noticing at the time
something remarkably nectarean in the taste. As I
supposed the evolutions which it had accomplished
in mid-air had imparted to it an unusual flavor, and
as I wanted to see the performance again, I immediately subscribed for one more of the same sort.
Again the question about the fly—again an affirmative, with a remark that the bigger the fly, the better
I should be pleased, supposing that thereby he
would, for my satisfaction, make it fly through some
new motions. I am satisfied that this time the fly
was larger than on the former occasion. I was still
unsatisfied ; another subscription, and another lemonade, but this time the entomological interrogation
was not propounded—he took the fly for granted,
and he was right. About this time the person who
came home with me last night made his appearance.
I shook hands with him at once, for I thought I
recognized him. I imagined that he was a man
who, seven years ago, licked me with a rawhide for

stealing his pippins and setting fire to his sugar-bush, and I was anxious to shake hands for old acquaintance sake. I beg now, however, to state that I am satisfied this impression was erroneous, for I have this morning a distinct recollection that the individual of pomological memory removed to Kansas, where he was first lynched for stealing a horse, and afterward chosen county treasurer and inspector of election. However, be that as it may, certain it is, that, at that particular moment, thinking I had fallen in with an old friend, I invited him to drink with me. He accepted, and presently he proposed punch, and made a remark about cobbler. Punch I had heard mentioned as the prince of good fellows, and I was anxious to make his acquaintance. Cobbler I had only heard of as a man of lapstones and leather aprons, and I did not particularly desire to know him. On receiving an introduction to Punch, I was amazed to find that he was not an individual but a drink—a luscious combination of fragrant ingredients. Although I was mistaken in the identity, I was pleased with him, and it may not be superfluous to remark that the more I saw of him, the more I wanted to see, and the more I did see. About this time I had *two* friends ; there were *two*

10

active little men behind the bar, each throwing from double-barrelled tumblers two streams of lemonade over his head, each with two flies in. There were two beer-pumps, each with two dozen handles, and the number of bottles and decanters was beyond computation. The floor rose up and down in wooden billows, and knocked my hat off. I attempted to remonstrate with floor, but at this juncture the floor clinched me; we had a long wrestle, and finally went down—floor on top. By a convulsive exertion I 'turned' the floor, got it under, and stood on it to keep it down; had some compunctions about striking a fallen enemy, but passion got the better of me, and I tried to kick the floor; floor kicked back, and threw sand-dust in my eyes; got away; wanted to get out doors, but the room had changed about so, that the door was over my head, and the bar, with the active little men, was nearly under my feet; was afraid I should walk over the little men, and break the bottles; stepped very carefully so as to avoid any such accident, and put my foot in the stove. Peter rescued me from the devouring element, and got me out of doors.

" Peter said he would see me home, and asked me where I lived; told him I was an elephant; made him understand that I could *show* him the place where I hung out, even if I couldn't tell him—so we started.

" We must have come through Chatham street, for I can remember seeing some one with a hammer, selling clothing. I know I wanted to go in and make some purchases. The ruling idea in my mind, at that moment, was, that the grey mare wanted a winter overcoat, the oxen a pair of striped pantaloons apiece, that the sow, and each of her tender offspring, ought to have a red jacket and a pair of spectacles, and that it was a matter of necessity and charity to purchase seven dozen hickory shirts to keep the blue-jays away from the apple-trees. I went in, and commenced bidding. I know I was not particular about prices, and that any opposition provoked me exceedingly—so much so that I bid twenty-three dollars for a second-hand pocket-handkerchief, because, when the auctioneer started it at ten cents, and I offered fifteen, a hook-nosed Jew bid three cents over me. Auction over at last; man with the hammer wanted me to pay up—found that I had bought three quarters of his stock, and hadn't money enough to settle the bill. I know I gave him all I had, and also my coat and neckerchief to make up the balance. I also have a distinct recollection of

calling him a Hebrew robber, upon which he
knocked me in the eye with his hammer, and followed up this declaration of hostilities by splitting
my nose with a yard-stick. We got out of doors,
and proceeded down town. On the corner of Cham-
bers street the Third Avenue Railroad squared off,
and knocked me down. Peter held me steady, while
I rebuked the offender in proper terms. The Third
Avenue Railroad took off its hat and apologized. I
forgave it.

"We went into a cellar; got in by a complicated
dive. I sat down at first on the piano, next on a
pile of oyster-shells, and, finally, by the aid of a
huge pair of whiskers, with a little Dutchman
behind them, deposited myself in a chair—on top
of Peter. Peter got out after a prolonged struggle;
place very hirsute; big beards on everybody; ten
parts of hair to one part Dutchman. My vision may
have been slightly deranged, but I am certain that
one diminutive German had two pairs of whiskers—
a moustache just over his eyes, and a four-foot yellow
beard which sprung from his teeth. We drank lager
bier.

"Peter quoted Shakspeare when the man said
"pay up," and insisted on singing an English chorus
to a Dutch song; company indignant, Peter very

valiant, but too few in number. Peter fought, Peter
kicked, Peter swore, Peter was overpowered, Peter
was elevated in the arms of four stout Dutchmen
above the heads of the company. Exit Peter,
through the window. In leaving the room myself, I,
too, received some uncalled-for aid, but finally
rejoined Peter on the side-walk above.

"I spied the mystic light which told me the Elephantine resort was close at hand—couldn't fetch
it—asked M. P.—he said if we'd tell him the address
he'd show us—tried to recollect it—couldn't exactly
make it out, but said at a venture, corner of Maiden
Lane and Canal street—officer indignant—we finally
found the place, tried to come up still so as to surprise you, but I am willing to admit that attempt to
be a partial failure; we reached the door at last; it
wouldn't open—Peter called it Sebastopol, and proposed that we should storm it—we resolved ourselves
into an attacking party of two, called to our aid a
twelve-feet plank as a battering-ram, and by hard
blows persuaded the door to yield—that broken
panel is a forcible example of the power of moral
suasion.

"When I remark that, judging from my present
sensations, I should imagine a six-horse-power threshing-machine to be in the height of successful

operation in my head, immediately over my eyes, there are perhaps some sympathizing persons in the room, who have experienced the same delicious sensation, and can therefore 'phancy my pheelinks.'"

The members of the club expressed themselves eminently satisfied with Mr. Cake's statement of his experience, and the Higholdboy requested that Mr. Cake should inscribe in the records the said experience, in order that it might not be lost to future generations. Mr. Cake promised to do so.

Mr. Spout, being seized with a fit of liberality, ordered punches for the company, and two of the same kind for Johnny Cake, which Johnny indignantly refused, saying that, if before his recent experience in wholesale dissipation, he had disliked alcoholic beverages, such were his feelings now, that the dislike amounted to an abhorrence. Mr. Spout said it was all right, as in such case he should drink them all himself.

Mr. Dropper remarked that some two or three years previously, when he first arrived from Cincinnati, and before he had became fully posted up in the various phases of unwhipped rascality in New York, he had, on one occasion, owing to his ignorance, got into the station-house.

A general sentiment as expressed was, that Mr. Dropper should state the history of the circumstance, or be immediately expelled from the club, and kicked down stairs, minus his coat, hat, and boots.

Mr. Dropper said that he found it impossible to resist the gentle persuasions of his companions.

" Fellow quadrupeds," said he, " soon after my arrival in this mass meeting of bricks and mortar, I read in a morning paper the announcement of an extraordinary gift enterprise, which some benevolent and philanthropic individual had set on foot, with the view of making everybody, in general, and himself, in particular, rich. I thought of the subject for several days. The idea of securing a farm of three hundred acres in New Jersey, all in first-rate condition, with houses, barns, and fences ready-made, at the moderate cost of a dollar, was rather agreeable than otherwise, and the more I reflected upon the matter, the more I became satisfied that such a bargain was a consummation most devoutly to be wished for. One night I went to bed thinking of the farm. Finally I fell asleep, and

> ' Sleeping I dreamed, love,
> Dreamed love of '——

seeing six cats, each with two tails, and each tail

eight feet long, and afterwards a seventh cat with

 a bob-tail. When I awoke in the morning, I attempted to inter-ᴘret my dream, and I readily found a mean-ing. 1 put the figures together in the order above—that is to say, six cats, two tails, eight feet long, one cat bob-tail, which latter, I thought, was equivalent to a nought, and I had the following result: 62810. I concluded that this was the lucky number which was to get the farm. I posted off immediately to the office of the gift enter-prise, and called for number 62810, and laid down my dollar. The dollar was accepted, and the ticket was handed me, done up in an envelope. I was con-fident of having the title deeds to the premises given me as soon as the drawing should take place, and as that event was set down for the next week, and there was no time to be lost, I contracted for thirty-two head of cattle, and all the necessary farming utensils, in order to be ready to commence a life of ease and luxury, at the earliest practicable moment,

after the said real estate should come into my possession. I also advertised for two stout farm-hands, to assist me in following the prospective agricultural pursuits. I had some three hundred and sixty-eight answers. I finally engaged two athletic Irishmen, who were recommended by their late employer as being excellent farm-hands, and who, in addition, possessed this virtue, that, when drunk, they were satisfied to abuse one another, and never their employer.

"The day of the drawing at last came, and I went to the office to get my deed, for I never doubted a single instant that I had drawn the big prize. I entered the office, and told the clerk that I would take the documents.

"'What documents?' said he.

"'Why, my deed of the magnificent country mansion and farm in New Jersey, with three hundred acres of land, and a house with all the modern improvements.'

"Gentlemen, I have been, in the course of my life, kicked by a horse, knocked into a cocked hat by a threshing-machine, and had my hair singed off by chain-lightning, but neither one of these occurrences so astounded me as did that red-haired clerk, when he informed me that my ticket had drawn a gold

10*

pen, with a silver holder, and a place in the top to put pencil-leads in.

"Gentlemen, I was not furious, I was perfectly cool; but when I jumped over that counter, and laid hands on that red-haired clerk, I will admit that it was my calmly-settled intention to eat that red-haired clerk for luncheon, notwithstanding his cock-eye. A hasty glance at the mud on his boots, and the metal buttons on his coat-tails, caused me to alter my original amiable intention, and I made up my mind to be gentle with him, and merely whip him so his mother wouldn't be able to tell him from a Little Neck clam on a large scale, and then leave him to live through it if he could.

"I struck him once, and he laid down in a corner among some bottles, with his head in the gas-meter, and in one minute from that time he was one universal damage.

"The proprietor being done for, I proceeded to demolish the establishment; I didn't leave, of the chairs, tables, and desks, a piece big enough to make a bird-cage, and having turned on all the gas, I was seriously debating whether I should not set the whole shop on fire, and sue for the insurance, when the two Irishmen, whom I had engaged to work my farm, made their appearance. I told them to clear out, to budge, move on, leave, but they evidently took me for a swindler, and were bound to pay me off. They pitched into me; our amiable struggle to put each other's eyes out attracted a crowd; the muss became general; everybody went in, and before the policemen came there was considerable music. Nobody was bashful, and the result was four interesting cases of black eye, a pathetic instance of demolished nose, two lovely examples of swelled head, an agreeable specimen of peeled shin, seven illustrations of the beautifying power of finger-nails, when forcibly applied to the physiognomy, and three convincing exemplifications of the power of the Irish fist in extracting opposing teeth, without the aid of forceps or turnkey. The police came at last, and arrested the entire multitude. That night we slept in the station-house. I don't want to say anything against the bunks in that station-house, but this I *do* say, that if there ever is a bed-bug convention, and that station-house is not well represented, it won't be because any lack of population deprives them of the right to a strong delegation; and if, at any national mass meeting of fleas, they stand in need of ten or fifteen thousand to make up a quorum, the station-house of that ward can supply them, without any perceptible decrease of its entomological census.

"In the morning we were conducted before the Justice, but as there were about forty cases to be heard before mine, I had ample leisure to look about, and take a realizing sense of the beauties of my situation. The case of myself and others was at length reached. The officers swore to the muss, as if the numerous broken heads were not sufficient evidence that there had been a difference of opinion. One of the Irishmen became a volunteer liar in his own behalf, but the Justice recognized him as an old customer, often brought up for drunkenness, and knowing him to be a reliable liar, he placed his evidence all to my credit, and discharged me without even a fine, but with the assurance that if I came there again he would 'send me up.' Not wanting to make any such equivocal ascension as a matter of experiment, I have kept away from him, and cut up all my subsequent monkey-shines in another ward, which is out of his jurisdiction."

After Mr. Dropper closed, there was a brief silence, in which each member quietly smoked his pipe, apparently reflecting upon the morals of lotteries. At last Wagstaff inquired who won the farm.

"I forgot that," resumed Dropper. "I learned from an advertisement which appeared in the daily journals, that ticket number 6281 drew the farm. This number, you will observe, corresponds with the one I supposed would be the lucky one, except that in mine a nought was annexed to the four figures, making it 62810, instead of 6281. My mistake grew out of a misinterpretation of my dream, in respect to the bob-tailed cat, I having assumed that the diminutive nether extremity, in this instance, was equivalent to a nought expressed, whereas, if I had let it remain a nought understood, and had acted accordingly, I should have been the lucky man."

"Not so lucky as you imagine," remarked Quackenbush, "for the facts of that matter I am somewhat familiar with. A country fiddler, living up in Connecticut, held the ticket which entitled the holder to the real estate aforesaid. He saw the advertisement, and I being the only acquaintance he had in the city, he wrote to me to secure the deeds, as he couldn't raise the money to come down. I called at the office of the managers of the enterprise, and presented the ticket. They said it was all right; congratulated me on the luck of my friend, and told me to call a week from that time, and they would be prepared to execute the deed. This I thought was very fair, and I left the office. On the appointed day I called, and found the office closed, as the managers had sloped."

The conversation then turned upon Police Courts, and the facilities which they afforded in aiding a person to get glimpses of the elephant. It was conceded that the experience of Dropper, just related, opened very fair, and, on the suggestion of Mr. Quackenbush, it was resolved :

1. That the members of the club do make it their business

2. To visit the Police Courts

3. Before the next meeting of the club.

The meeting was adjourned by the club, singing, " We're all jolly good fellows."

The Police Courts.

"I do remember Ann—"
A. POTHECARIE.

Several evenings
passed before all the
members of the club
again assembled. In
the meantime the
quantity of manu-
scripts had become
unusually large, the
members   having
found that the Police

Courts were prolific in sights of the colossal quadruped.   When they did meet it was whispered that one
of the members had had some personal experience, not
only as a spectator but as a prisoner.   No questions,
however, were propounded upon the subject, in a
tone loud enough for the member in question to hear,
as they desired to allow him to speak of the matter
voluntarily, confess his fault, and receive the forgiveness of his fellows.

The proceedings of the evening were opened by the
Higholdboy, who took his official seat, announced
that the special order of the meeting was to hear the
reports of members who had been present at the
sessions of the Police Courts, with the view of noting
down their zoölogical features.

The Higholdboy called upon Dennis, Wagstaff, and
Overdale for the result of their visit to the Police
Courts.   Wagstaff's note-book was produced, and
the lengthened narratives inscribed therein went to
show the following state of facts.

Wagstaff arose one morning at six precisely, and,
after having hit Dennis with his own wooden leg, and
pulled Overdale's eyes open by his whiskers and hair,
announced to them if they were going to visit the Essex
Market Police Court that day, to see the animals, that
it was time to rise.   They slipped on their clothing

as soon as possible, and started somewhat sooner. They passed the Odd Fellows Hall, which Overdale expatiated upon at some length as an extensive log-chain factory. He formed his conclusion from seeing three links of chain represented in a conspicuous part of the building. The Westchester House he informed them was Washington's head quarters, and under this belief they stopped some time to look at it, and speak of it in connection with the many stories related of that interesting relic of the architecture of the last century.

They arrived at length at the Essex Market, in the upper part of which the police magistrate of that judicial district sits in a big chair, for the purpose of dealing out retail justice and getting a wholesale living.

The trio ascended into the court-room, where the justice was seated, disposing of the hard cases which had accumulated during the night. Overdale was still communicative. In answer to the inquiries of Dennis, he informed that gentleman that the police clerks were associated justices, that the prisoner's cage was the jury-box, and pointed out the prisoners themselves as the jury. The humble member of the police, who is known as the doorman, Overdale said answered well the description of the Chief of the Police, contained in one of the historic works of John

McLenan. Dennis inquired where the prisoners were.
Overdale was unable to answer, but at last expressed
it as his opinion that the persons who were standing
about them must "be the malefactors." Dennis
said he never could satisfactorily account for the
jurors being tried, and sent out of the room in charge
of officers, but he had too much confidence in the
extensive knowledge and vast intelligence of Overdale, to suppose that his hirsute friend could possibly
be mistaken. In consequence of this misplaced confidence on the part of Wagstaff and Dennis, the note-
book of the former was filled with notes of the trials
of the different members of the jury.

One case of which Wagstaff took full notes, was
that of Edward Bobber, a seafaring man, of very
peculiar appearance, possessing some remarkable
characteristics of manner, dress, speech, looks, and
action. He was charged with being drunk. In
the way of physical beauty, Edward was decidedly
a damaged article. He had lost one arm by a
snake-bite, and been deprived of an eye by the
premature explosion of a pistol, which broke his
spectacles at the same time it extinguished his sinister optic. The unexpected descent of a ship-mate,
from the tops, upon his head, had turned his neck so
that he seemed to be keeping a perpetual look out
over his shoulder with his remaining eye. His nose

resembled a half-ripe tomato, and a pair of warty excrescences hung upon his face, as if some one had shot a couple of marbles at him, which had stuck to him for life. His complexion bore a close resemblance to the outside of a huckleberry-pudding. His teeth, which were unusually long, projected backward, as if they had taken a start to grow down his throat. This last peculiarity was, undoubtedly, one cause of a remarkable singularity of speech, which seriously impaired his natural facility of conversation. Some idiosyncrasy of disposition, probably, had also something to do with this lingual embarrassment, but certain it is, that Mr. Edward Bobber never answered one question until he was asked another, to which last he would give the reply intended for query number one. Whether his mental faculties needed always a second-interrogative punching up, or whether the fangs projecting downward retained one answer until displaced by another, Wagstaff and his friends were unable to decide; but they truly believe that an inquiry propounded to Edward Bobber, aforesaid, would have remained unanswered until doomsday, unless a second question followed the first.

A transcript of a conversation between him and the Clerk of the Court reads as follows:

"*Clerk.*—Where were you born?

"The prisoner removed his solitary orb from its guardianship, over his left shirt sleeve, rolled it slowly round until it commanded a fair view of the questioner, but said nothing. The clerk, nothing daunted, continued:

" ' How long have you been in this country ?'

"The face assumed a look of intelligence, and answer No. 1 came out.

"*Edward.*—Broome County.

"*Clerk.*—How old are you ?

"*Edward.*—Two years.

"*Clerk.*—How long have you been drunk ?"

"*Edward.*—Thirty-four years, seven months, and nine days.

"*Clerk.*—Where did you get your liquor ?

"*Edward* (rolling his eye toward the Judge).-- Been on a spree four days.

"*Judge* (very indignant).—Did you say I've been on a spree?

"*Edward.*—Old Mother Bidwell's, down in Mott street.

"*Clerk.*—Do you mean hereafter to treat this Court respectfully ?

"*Edward.*—No, sir; I hope not.

"*Officer with red hair.*—If you ain't crazy, I'm a jack-ass.

"*Edward.*—Yes, sir, of course.

" The excited Judge here commenced making out his commitment, but the Clerk, who began to see the fun, thought best to ask him a few more questions first, and accordingly inquired of Bobber what he traded in, as he seemed to own a sloop. The prisoner, who had been cogitating upon the last remark of the red-haired officer until he had waxed wroth, burst out :

" ' Jack-ass! jack-ass! yes, you *are* a jack-ass ; not a doubt of it.'

"*Clerk.*—Come, tell me what kind of liquor did you drink yesterday ?

"*Edward.*—Soap, candles, coffee, bar-lead, chickens, coal, pine kindling-wood, smoked hams, and white-wood shingles—

"*Judge* (interfering).—Prisoner, you are only getting yourself into trouble. My patience will give out. I can't stand everything. Do you think I'm made of patience ?

" *Edward.*—Whisky ; nothing but whisky, sir ; upon my honor.

" The last answer proved too much for the gravity of the Court. The Judge, the Clerk, the attendant officers, and all smiled audibly. A whispered word from the Clerk explained to the Justice the true state of the case. Edward was discharged, and as he

departed from the court-room, an officer, two blocks
away, heard him, in answer to a request for a penny
proffered by a little girl, give what was undoubtedly
intended as a detailed reply to the last interrogative
remark of the Police Justice."

The case of Mr. Palmerston Hook, which was also
reported in Wagstaff's note-book, would seem to
indicate that there was more than one way of catch-
ing fish.

"Mr. Hook was brought up as a vagrant. He was
a smooth-faced individual, about old enough to vote,
dressed in rather grotesque, flashy clothes, very
much worn. The sleeves of his coat were quite
large, in accordance with the prevailing style. But
they served a purpose of utility, as was developed
by the evidence, in a rather novel profession which
Mr. Hook followed.

"The principal witness was Mr. James Skinner, a
very respectable dealer in Catherine Market, who
devotes his time and talents to purchasing eels from
the catchers thereof and selling the same to citizens
and others who desire to enjoy the luxury of eating
eels, either fried or done up in the form of pie or any
other form. Mr. Skinner has obtained for himself
an enviable popularity as a man of integrity. It has
never been said of him that he ever sold an eel

whose recent advent upon dry land from the salt water was a matter of serious question; and to think that Mr. Palmerston Hook should have selected Mr. Skinner's stock to depredate upon is a matter of some surprise. Mr. Skinner testified as follows:

"'This 'ere feller came to my eel-stand yes'day mornin' and asked me how eels was? Sez I, 'Good as usu'l,' and I axed him if he wanted to buy. Sez he, 'How much?' Says I, 'Eight'n pence.' Sez he, 'Is them all yer got?' Sez I, 'Yis.' Ye see, jest before this feller come up, I counted 'em and there was 'zactly 'lev'n. Then this 'ere feller he 'gun to paw 'em over, and kinder jumble 'em up together, which I thowt was wery funny; and at last, sez he, 'Guess I won't take none this mornin'.' He acted so kinder sneakin' that I thowt he wasn't all right, and 'fore he got out of sight I counted the eels an' found one on 'em was missen. I put for this 'ere feller and ketched him at the corner, an' I found my 'spicions was right, for on searchin' the chap I found a neel up in 'is coat-sleeve.'

"*Judge.*—How did he keep the eel up in his sleeve?

"*Mr. Skinner.*—Well, that was done in a kinder 'genus way; he had a fish'ook on the end of a line, an' the line was run up the right coat-sleeve, over

'is shoulder, an' it come down inside of 'is coat on
the left side, an' he come up to the stand, an' wen
he was a kinder pawin' over the eels he was a
ketchin' the fish'ook in the tail of the eel, an' as
soon as it was ketched in he pulled the line with his
left 'and an' drawed the eel up inter 'is sleeve ; an'
as soon as it was drawed up he stopped pawin' an'
left, an' 'ere's the fish'ook an' line wot I found on
'im ; an' I think he oughter be sent to Blackwell's
Island for bein' a wagrant.

"*Judge.*—Hook, what have you got to say for yourself ?

"*Mr. Hook.*—I 'aven't got nothin' to say honly I
vos wery 'ungry and vas a lookin' along in the market ven I 'appened to see the heels vot this 'ere hold
cock 'ad. Sez I to m'self, sez I, now, I'll hax the
price and mebbee the hole voman may vant von if
they's cheap. Vell, I 'appened t'ave a 'ook and
line in my coat, vich I spose haccidentally got
ketched in von of the heels, and ven I left to go and
tell the hole voman 'ow cheap they vas, it 'ung on
to the 'ook.

"*Judge.*—That's a pretty story to tell me. Do you
suppose I am going to believe it ?

"*Mr. Hook.*—On the honor of a gentleman that
vas the vay it 'appened.

"*Judge.*—At any rate, I shall send you up for three months.

"*Mr. Hook.*—Bust me, I honly vish you 'ad to try it three months yourself, you vouldn't think it vas quite so funny.

"Mr. Palmerston Hook was conducted below.

"Another interesting feature of the proceedings during the morning grew out of the case of Mr. Wallabout Warbler, whose name was the last called.

"Mr. Warbler had reached the last stages of shabby gentility. Time had told sadly on his garments, originally of fine material and fashionable cut. His black, curly hair was whitened out by contact with whitewash, and his nose had become a garden for the culture of blossoms by far more common than they are proper. But Mr. Warbler, despite the reverses which he had evidently suffered, stood proudly and gracefully erect. If the external man was in a state of dilapidation, the spirit still was unhurt. He smiled gracefully when the Judge addressed him and told him that he was charged with having been arrested in a state of drunkenness.

"Officers Clinch and Holdem were the witnesses against Mr. Warbler. They stated substantially that about one o'clock that morning they found Mr. Warbler standing in a garbage-barrel, on the edge

11

of the sidewalk, extemporizing doggerel to an imagi
nary audience. They insisted upon his stopping,
when Mr. Warbler told them that it was a violation
of etiquette to interrupt a gentleman when he was
delivering a poem before the alumni of a college.
He was evidently under the influence of liquor, and
quite out of his mind. They thought, for his own
safety, that they had better bring him to the station-
house.

"*Judge.*—Mr. Warbler, you have heard what the
officers have stated about your eccentric course of
conduct; how did you happen to get drunk?

"*Mr. Warbler.*—'Twas night, and gloomy darkness
had her ebon veil unfurled, and nought remained
but gas-lamps to light up this 'ere world. The
heavens frowned; the twinkling orbs, with silvery
light endowed, were all occult on t'other side a
thunderin' big black cloud. Pale Luna, too, shed
not her beams upon the motley groups which lazily
were standing round like new disbanded troops—

"*Judge.*—It's not to hear such nonsense that I occupy this seat—

"*Mr. Warbler.*—A death-like stillness e'er prevailed
on alley, pier and street.

"*Judge.*—To listen to such stuff, sir, I can't sacri-
fice my time—

"*Mr. W.*—Don't discombobilate my thought and interrupt my rhyme; I think that when misfortune is put on its defence, poetic justice, logic, law, as well as common sense, demand its story all be heard, unless *ex parte* proof is to send poor friendless cusses underneath the prison's roof. Shall I proceed?

"*Judge.*—Proceed; but don't make your tale too long.

"*Mr. W.*—I'll heed your words, depend upon't. I own that I was wrong in rushing headlong as I did into inebriation, but let me question now the Court; is it not a palliation of the depth of human guilt if malice don't incite to break in divers fragments State laws wrong or right, and when only human appetite, uncontrolled by human reason leads men of genius, oftentime, the dish of life to season with condiments which *pro tem.* the mental palate tickle, yet very often, in the end, put human joys in pickle which ain't so cussed funny; though all of the expense of grub and the *et ceteras* the public pays for; hence, I ask this Court (believing that its feelings are not hampered) if justice should not ever be with human mercy tempered?

"*Judge.*—Perhaps. Now, tell me, Warbler, where you bought your liquor.

"*Mr. W.*—Anon I'll tell you. Last week, Judge,

prostrate was I, far sicker than to me's agreeable,
with the diarrhea chronic, and sympathizing friends
advised that I should take some tonic. I asked
them what: at once they said, ' Get some lager-bier.'
'Twas got. ' Drink freely, boy,' said they, ' nothing
need you fear, but you'll be up and on your legs.'
The lager-bier ' was took ;' soon every object in my
sight had a very drunken look. Lager-bier (to German ears the words may be euphonic.) Tonic, certainly, it was, but decidedly too—tonic. Abnormal
thirst excited it, and I went to great excesses (the
statement's quite superfluous, my nose the fact con-
fesses). Last night, attracted by the scenes which
Gotham's streets present, I dressed myself in sombre
clothes, and out of doors I went; to quench my
thirst did I imbibe the more of lager-bier at Hoff-
man's on the corner, several squares from here. No
more know I, 'cept in the morn I wakened from my
sleep, and having sowed, perhaps I'll learn that like-
wise I must reap.

" *Judge.*—Have you got ten dollars ?

"*Mr. W.*—'Tis true, I hain't a red ; I suppose the
words unpleasant which next to me'll be said ; that
because by my imprudence my pocket-book's collapsed, in prison drear must I remain till ten days
have elapsed.

"*Judge.*—I'll let you go this time.

"*Mr. Warbler.*—Ha, say you so? Is't true, that though my offence is rank, in vain I did not sue for mercy; ne'er 'll I fail to say both through thin and thick in the circle of my acquaintance that you're a perfect brick.

" Mr. Wallabout Warbler left the room."

Mr. Van Dam announced that he had visited the Jefferson Market Police Court one morning, and though there was much in the proceedings that was uninteresting, he had yet been able to collate some facts which he doubted not would be regarded as worthy of being recorded upon the minutes of the club.

After taking a punch, Mr. Van Dam proceeded.

He stated that a dozen or two individuals, all of whom, not having the fear of the law before their eyes, and being instigated by a morbid thirst, and who did in the city and county of New York drink, swill, imbibe, smile, guzzle, suck, and pour down various spirituous, fermented, or malt liquors, wine, beer, ale or cider, and from the effects thereof did get drunk, were severally favored with moral lectures and ten dollar fines. The first were not appreciated, and the second were not paid.

But the case which interested Mr. Van Dam

most was that of four boys, named Frederick T. White, Michael Keefe, John Wheeler, and Manning Hough, who were arraigned on a charge of disorderly conduct. They were bright-looking boys of about thirteen years of age, dressed in plain but neat clothes, and with the exception of White, did not seem much to like the position they occupied. There was a devil-may-care, though not a vicious look, about White, which was positively refreshing. He seemed to rather like the position than otherwise, and from a roguish leer that was observed in his eye as he surveyed a personage who was to appear as the witness against him, Mr Van Dam was led to anticipate something in the shape of novelty, and he accordingly prepared for the worst. The Judge told the boys the nature of the charge against them. The name of the witness being called, Mr. Conrad Heinrich Holzenkamp announced his presence by an emphatic ' Here.'

Mr. Holzenkamp was a man who was the very ideal of a lager bier saloon keeper. His weight was at least two hundred and seventy-five pounds, one half of which could be set down to lager bier. His height was not more than five feet eight, but the circumference and diameter of the lager bier were enormous. He carried himself erect by necessity to balance the lager bier in the front. His hide was in wrinkles across the back of his neck whenever he held back his head, and every wrinkle seemed ready to burst with lager bier. Mr. Holzenkamp's face looked lager bier ; Mr. Holzenkamp walked lager bier, drank and ate lager bier in alternation. He thought lager bier, dreamed lager bier. In brief, Mr. Holzenkamp was composed of two things: first, the effects of lager bier; and second, lager bier.

Mr. Blotter, the clerk, administered the oath in his characteristic manner as follows:

" You solemnly swear, in the presence of Almighty God, that the evidence which you shall give in the present case, shall be the truth, the whole truth, and nothing but the truth, so help you God, kiss the book, and get out of my way.

" *Mr. Holzenkamp.*—I can shwear to all de dings vat you shpeak, but to tell de whole troot, dat can I not shwear; ven I can dinks fon all dese boys have done, I tells you more as genuff to sends them to de Benidentiary for so long as dey lives; a hoonerd dings dey do vot I dinks not of.

"*The Court.*—Kiss the book, Mr. Holzenkamp.

" The witness proceeded to bring a gill of lager bier contained in his nose, and a half gill of lager bier contained in his lips, in contact with a venerable

Bible, which has been so familiar with crime by long association that we almost wonder the text has not been long since corrupted as much as the cover. Lager bier and the Bible having come in contact, lager bier is supposed to be incapable of lying.

"*The Court.*—Mr. Holzenkamp, please state the circumstances connected with the arrest of these boys.

"*Mr. H.*—Vell, on Vensday night, at von o'clock, my koostumers dey all goes vay fom mine lager bier, saloon, und I say to Yawcob to go mit him and put up de blinds; ven he goes out mineself, mine vife, ve drinks some lager bier, and den I dakes de money and counts dem and puts dem in mine pocket; ven Yawcob come in ve locks de door, and goes de shtairs up to shleep; vel mine vife and I get to de bed in, so soon as ve can, and den I shleeps; ven I bin shleep leetle vile mine vife she shakes me and say, 'Heinrich, de cats dey makes noise in de shtreets so dat I cannot shleep;' ven I vakes up I hear so much cats squall in de shtreets dat I dinks dere vas a meetin fon cat politicians. But dey makes so much noise I cannot vink mine eyes vonce to shleep; so I get up and goes to de window and say 'shcat,' 'shcat;' but de more I say shcat de more dey vill not shcat.

I say to mine vife, 'Katrina, you bin so younger and so smaller as I bin, you go down in de shtreets and drives 'vay de cats.' My vife den goes down, and ven she opens de door de cat squalls not more, and she looks to see dem, but dere is not cats in de shtreets. Ven she comes de shtairs up again and say de cats bin gone ve lie on de bed to shleep; vell, ven I bin yust shleep most, mine Gott! I hear de cats so louder as before, and I say to mine vife all de cats in de city bin come on the shtep-valk fon mine lager bier saloon; dey squall like hoonerd dyvels, and I try more to shcat dem vay. But it was no goot; dey shquall—I cannot say to you so bad as dey shquall. Mine vife say dere bin a tunder-shower fon cats; ven I lie in mine bed and shtand it so long as I can, I jump up und shwear dat I shoots all de cats in de vorld; I dakes mine bistol and runs de shtairs down, but I bin so mad, und I go so quick, dat I falls the shtairs over, und in a minute finds mine head knock on de vall, my right hand in some Schweitzer cheese, de oder in de shpit-box, und von foot in de big ice-pitcher; so soon as I can gits up and goes to de door und opens it, I goes on de shtep-valk, und mine foot shlips, and I falls down on mine back, and breaks all de bones in mine body; I feels mine hand on de shtep-valk, and I find it bin all covered mit

11*

soft soap; I dries to raise mineself, but I bin so
heavy dat I down falls before I get up; yust den
mine vife come and help me, and bulls me fom de
shtep-valk in de door; ve do not hear de cats den,
und so ve goes to de beds again; so soon as ve lie
down I hears de cats so vorse as de oder time—I
hears notings but cats; I never was so much afraid
except vonce ven a lager bier barrel fly in bieces; I
goes to de vindow and I dinks I hear dem on de awning, und I gets out; yust den de cats shtop, but I
say I vill find vere dey bin on de awning; I valk
along und my foot trips on some shtrings, and ven I
fall I hear one loud cat-shquall dat fright me so dat
I dinks I bin fall on more as dhree hoonered cats;
ven I can get up I feels on de shtrings, und I valks
till I finds a box; I brings de box to de vindow;
Katrina gets de lamp und dere ve find in de long
vood shoe-box seven cats vat vas fixed dis way:
seven notch holes vas cut in de side de box, and de
cats was put in de box mit deir heads shtick out de
holes; on de oder side de box was seven leetle notch
holes vere vas de cats' dails, und a shtring vas tie to
all de cats' dails; I know dat de cats come not in de
box by demselves, und so I look to see vere vas de
boys; I comes de shtairs down again, goes on de
shtep-valk so soft as I can, and I finds vere de strings

comes down fom de awning; I keeps hold de shtring till I find it come to a big sugar hogshead by de next house, and dere I find dese boys; yust den I say 'Vatch!' and de boliceman comes and dakes de boys to de station-house; I believe dey is de same boys as trouble me before.

" *The Court.*—Boys, what have you got to say for yourselves for such conduct?

"Master White volunteered to act as spokesman. He said:

" Well, one day we was a playing in front of this 'ere man's lager bier saloon, and he come out and threatened to lick us if we didn't stop. We kept on, and bine-by he comes to the door when we wasn't a lookin', and threw a pailful of dirty water on us. We thought we'd got as good a right to the street as he had, so we made up our minds to be even with him, and we got the box and cats and serenaded him.

" Mr. Holzenkamp stated that he baptized the boys a few days before as described. The boys promised not to bother lager bier saloon keepers any more, in consideration of which they were discharged."

Mr. Van Dam stated that the last case called was that of Mr. Timothy O'Neil.

The case he said occupied the attention of the

court nearly a half hour, owing to the difficulty which the court experienced in getting him to make direct responses to his questions.

"Timothy appeared in a grey dress-coat—that is to say, it was high in the waist, with a short and pointed tail, a feature oftener produced by tailors than by literary men of the present day. Timothy's vest was red; his breeches were made of corduroy. Below them were long coarse stockings and brogans.

"The evidence went to show that Timothy had been found drunk in the street, but he was not communicative on the subject. He did not call the officer a liar after he had heard him give his evidence, nor tell the judge that he was an 'owld tief.' He said nothing until he was asked to take the usual oath. The Judge said: 'Mr. O'Neil, put your hand on the book.' Mr. O'Neil complied cautiously, fearing the result of his act. When the words of the oath were uttered he made the sign of the cross, and after being requested by the court, kissed the Bible.

" *The Clerk.*—What's your name?

" *Prisoner.*—The same as me father's.

" 'What was his name?'

" 'The same as mine.'

" 'Tell me your name or you shall be locked up.'

" 'Timothy.'

" ' And what else ?'

" ' I haven't any middle name.'

" ' I mean your last name.'

" ' O'Neil.'

" ' How long have you been in the city ?'

" ' Since I come to the counthry.'

" ' How long is that ?'

" ' Pat Hooligan can tell ye betther nor I can.'

" ' What month was it ?'

" ' The first Sunday in Lint.'

" ' Where do you live ?'

" ' Wid Biddy and the childer.'

" ' Where do they live ?'

" ' The second floor, back room, bad luck to the bugs that's in it.'

" ' I mean what street ?'

" ' Mike Henessy's store is on the first floor.'

" ' Tell me what street the house is on ?'

" ' Who the divil can tell whin they are changin' the names of the blackguard streets so much ?'

" ' What was the street called before the name was changed ?'

" ' Anthony street; they calls it by another name now.'

" ' Worth street I suppose you mean ?'

" ' I mane that the painter should have put it Worthless street.'

" ' Whereabouts in Worth street ?'

" ' Three doors from the corner.'

" ' What corner ?'

" ' The corner of the street.'

" ' What street ?'

" ' The street three doors above.'

" ' Well what is its name ?'

" ' Bad luck to you, why didn't ye ax me that before ?'

" ' Well, tell me the name.'

" ' Faith I don't know miself.   It's an alley.'

" ' Well, what's the number of the house ?'

" ' The number on the door do you mane ?'

" ' Certainly.'

" ' There isn't anny.'

" ' What is your trade ?'

" ' Me father never 'prenticed me.

" ' I mean what do you work at ?'

" ' I don't do any work.'

" ' Why ?'

" ' Because you've got me locked up in prison.'

" ' Will you tell me what you work at when out of prison ?'

" ' I'm a laborin' man, sir '

" ' At what were you employed?'

" ' Haird work.'

" ' What kind of work?'

" ' In the shores' (sewers).

" ' You are charged with being drunk.'

" ' Dhrunk, is it. Faith, I never was more sober in my life than I am at this minute.'

" ' That may be; but here are a half-dozen men who are ready to swear that they saw you drunk yesterday.'

" ' Av it comes to that, can't I bring twiste as manny who will swear that they didn't see me dhrunk yisterday.'

" ' What kind of liquor did you drink?'

" ' Mighty bad liquor, and ye'd say the same av ye was to thry it.'

" ' Was it malt or spirituous liquor?'

" ' It was nayther; it was whisky.'

" ' Where did you purchase it?'

" ' At the Dutchman's.'

" ' Where is his store?'

" ' On the corner.'

" ' What corner?'

" ' The corner nearest to where they're buildin' the shtore.'

" ' Where is that?'

" ' Where I was workin'.'

" *The Court.*—What was O'Neil doing when you found him ?

" *Officer.*—He was lying very drunk in a hole which he had been digging.

"*Prisoner.*—Be me sowl you're wrong for wonst; I didn't dig the howl; I dug out the dirt and left the howl.

" ' Were you ever up before the Court before ?'

" ' No, nor behind aither; when I want to be again, I'll sind to your honor and let ye know.'

" ' If I let you off this time will you keep sober ?'

" ' Faith I will, unliss the Dutchmin keep betther liquor nor they do now.'

" ' You may go.'

" ' Thank ye, sir—ye're a gintleman, av there iver was wan.'

" Mr. Timothy O Neil left the court-room."

Mr. Dropper also proposed to relate the experience of some half a dozen mornings which he had spent in the pursuit of amusement under difficulties, when he had occupied himself in seeing the sights around the Jefferson Market Police Court.

" On one of the mornings which I devoted to visiting the Tombs," said Mr. Dropper, " the class of prisoners varied.   Most of them claimed to be from

the western of the British Isles. Others said they
were born in Cork, Clare, Down, and other counties.
A number answered to patronymics to which were
prefixed the letter O, and an apostrophe. One party,
who called themselves Fardowners, looked brick-bats
at another party who occupied a remote corner of
the cage, and who claimed to be Connaughtmen.
the remainder of the prisoners were Irish.

"An interesting feature in the proceedings of the
morning was a case in which Owen Shaughnessy,
Patrick Mulholland, Michael O'Shea, Timothy Leahey, Dennis Maroney, Dermot McDermott, Phelim
Flannegan, Bridget O'Keefe, Mary McBride, Ellen
Dougherty and Bridget Casey were the defendants.
As the Judge called out their names, the prisoners
severally responded. They were all, as their names
would indicate, of Irish birth. The men, evidently
long-shoremen and laborers, and the women, servants.
Their garments, in some instances, were torn, and in
other ways disarranged and soiled. The men, and
in one or two instances the women, showed bruises
about their faces and hands, indicating their active
participation in a recent scrimmage, from the effects
of which they had not had the time, or soap and
water, to enable them to recover.

"Mr. Gerald O'Grady, who stands at the head of

the bar at the Tombs, and who, under adverse circumstances and strong competition, has been enabled, by his talents, to keep up his tariff of fees, from which he has never deviated, appeared as counsel for the prisoners. Mr. O'Grady has never been known to defend a case for less than fifty cents, unless, actuated by feelings of commendable philanthropy, he has volunteered his professional services gratis. It may be reasonably supposed that his success has excited the envy of the 'shysters;' for while they have to sit oftentimes a whole morning beside their respective granite columns at the Tombs, without being called upon to defend a case, Mr. O'Grady's presence in the court-room is in frequent demand. Mr. O'Grady had been retained in this case, I learned, by seven of the defendants, at a certain specified fee for each man, he volunteering his professional services to the ladies without charge. He announced to the Court that he represented the defendants, and that they were ready to have the trial commence.

" 'Is Mr. O'Grady your counsel?' the Judge inquired of the defendants.

" 'Yes, yer honor,' said one of the parties addressed; 'didn't I pay him five shillings—divil a hap'ny less—for to defind me.'

" 'Five shillings ?' said Mr. O'Grady, indignantly, ' you mane that as a retainer, of coorse.'

"*Defendant.*—I mane that's all ye'll get, anny how——

"*Counsel* (loudly).—Say, sir, it is time for you to know that, as a client, you should addhress the Coort only through your counsel. (To the Court.) Sir, my clients here, paceable citizens, stand ready for to answer, through me, to the diabolical chairges which designin' min have brought against thim, feelin' within their breasts—— (Here Mr. O'Grady hit one of his clients a severe blow in his bread-basket).

"*Assaulted Client.*—Oh! h–h—.

" *Counsel* (to client).—Keep your mouth shut, why don't you ? (To the Court.) Feelin', as I said before, widthin their breasts, the proud conscious-ness of their entire innocence of anny charges which their accusers could dare for to bring against thim.

" The witnesses were Sergeant Ferrett and Officers Snap, Catcher, O'Grasp, Ketchum, Holder, and Van Knabem.

" Officer Holder stated, in substance, that while patrolling his beat during Thursday night, the in-mates of a house, No. 83½ Pacific Place, began to get very disorderly. From the howlings and noises

which he heard, he came to the conclusion that
there was a wake in the house. Not desiring to
stop the disturbance by any violent means, he
knocked at the door, with the view of telling them
that they were disturbing the public peace, and
requesting them to desist. No response was made
to his knock. He then put his mouth to the key-
hole of the door, and announced to them, as audibly
as he could, that unless they desisted, he should have
to call other officers and arrest them. No attention
was paid to his words. Sergeant Ferrett arrived
soon after, and inasmuch as the disturbance continued to increase, they called in the other officers to
make a descent on the place, not, however, until
they had first endeavored, by their voices, to make
the inmates of the house understand the consequence
to them, in case they persisted in their unlawful
course. Officer Ketchum, who had formerly patrolled
the beat, knew of a rear entrance to the house
through an alley, and they accordingly entered the
house by that way. They found about twenty persons present, men and women, engaged in a promiscuous scrimmage, howling, drinking, and fighting.
The orders of the sergeant to cease their disturbance
did not avail anything, which decided them to arrest
the leading actors in the scene, which they forthwith

accomplished, after some considerable resistance on
the part of the company. They brought them to
the station-house. The remainder of the party subsequently retired or left the place, which was quiet
for the rest of the night.

"The remaining officers confirmed the evidence
of officer Holder, in such of its particulars as they
were acquainted with. All of them were cross-
questioned, more or less, by Mr. O'Grady, without,
however, eliciting any new facts of material interest.

"Mr. O'Grady introduced, as a witness for the
defense, Mrs. Katheleen Hennesy.

"Mrs. Hennesy is a lady of about forty-five years
of age, five feet ten inches in height, weighing about
two hundred and fifty pounds. She has a florid face.
Her dress was remarkable for the extent with which
it was ornamented with highly-colored ribbons and
laces, gathered in fantastic bows.

"Mr. Blotter, the clerk, administered the usual
oath.

"Mrs. Hennesy, having kissed the book, the
examination was commenced.

"*Mr. O'Grady.*—Misthress Hennesy, will you state
to the Coort if you're the proprietor of the house No.
83½ Pacific Place.

"*Mrs. Hennesy.*—Av coorse I am, and divil a

hap'ny is there owin' to anny man for what's inside of it.

"*Mr. O'G.*—What kind of a house do you keep there ?

"*Mrs. H.*—Is it for to prove that the charackther of me house is not good that yer afther axin' the question ?

"*Mr. O'G.*—Misthress Hennesy, could ye make it convanient to thrate this Coort wid becoming respect, by answerin' the questions that I put to ye, for the purpose of establishin' a definse of these ladies and gintlemen, some of whom, I am towld, are inmates of yer house ? What kind of a house, I'll ax ye wonst more, do ye keep ?

"*Mrs. H.*—It's a respectable, honest boordin'-house ; bad luck to the blackgaird that says it's not.

"*Mr. O'G.*—Will you plase to state to the Coort the facts of the unfortunate occurrence that thran-spired in yer house last night ?

"*Mrs. H.*—For the matther o' that, there's mighty little for to tell ; for it was nothin' more nor a wake, barrin' that the corpse come to life widout showin' the civility of first tellin' the mourners that he wasn't dead at all at all, and sayin', ' By yer lave, I'd rather not be, av it's all the same to yez.'

"*Mr. O'G.*—It's about that, Misthress Hennesy,

that his honor is a waitin' for ye to spake of. Now, thin, will ye relate the facts?

"*Mrs. H.*—Well, plase yer honor, it was yestherday mornin' airly that I heard Timothy Garretty was up stairs in his room, very sick, and like to die. I dhressed myself, and sent for the docther, and went up stairs; and throth Tim was a lyin' there in wan of his fits, wid which he had been often throubled before; and before the docther could come to him, the circulation of his brathin' had stopped entirely. Well, yer honor, Tim had manny frinds in the house, and as he was an owld boordher, we thought to howld a wake over his body. He was laid out, and put into a coffin. At night all of his frinds come into the room, where everything was illegantly arranged for the wake. They had begun to dhrink their whisky, and was enjoyin' themselves in a gintale way, whin Pat Mulholland, he sthruck Mike O'Shea over the eye for somethin' that Mike had said, and wid that Mike's frinds and Pat's frinds got themselves mixed up in a free fight together. At that time, plase yer honor, who should I see arisin' from the coffin but Timothy Garretty himself, and restin' on his hands. By my sowl I was freckened, for I thought it was Tim's apparition that was appearin'. Thin Tim spoke up; 'Bad luck to yez,'

says he, 'isn't it a fine thing yez is doin'—havin' the whisky flowin' free, and a free fight, too, and keepin' me a lyin' in this blackgaird box on the broad of me back, widout ever so much as axin' me if I had a mouth on me at all at all?' Wid that somebody who was a strikin' happened to hit Timothy a clout in the eye, which knocked him back into the coffin.

"'Who the divil did that?' sez Tim, as he made a spring from the coffin on to the floor, dhressed all up in his white clothes. 'Show me the man that shtruck me in me eye;' and wid that Tim he commenced a shtrikin' out, and he shtruck Dennis Marony under the but of the lug. Whin they saw Tim out of his coffin, they stopped a fightin', and fell on their knees, and commenced a sayin' their prayers. 'What's the matther wid yez?' says Tim.

"'Are ye not dead?' says Larry O'Brien.

"'Yes, as dead as a nest of live flaze,' says Tim.

"'Then yer alive,' says they.

"'Thry me wid some whisky,' says he; and wid that they got up and give Tim some whisky, which he never dhrank wid a betther grace nor thin. Well, as Tim wasn't dead, they couldn't howld the wake, but they said it would be a pity to lave the whisky to spoil, so they agreed that they'd have the spree just the same. Tim was purty wake from his fit, and so it didn't take long to make him dead dhrunk, whin we laid him in his bed. Afther that, yer honor, they kept on a dhrinkin', and was fightin' in the most frindly way, whin the M. P.s come into the door, and tuck some of thim off to the station-house. I thin shut up the house, and the rest wint to bed.

"*Judge.*—Mrs. Hennesy, where is Timothy, the corpse?

"'Here, sir,' said a cadaverous-looking Hibernian, 'a little the worse for dyin' widout bein' very dead.'

"*Judge.*—I think you're good for a few years yet if you take care of yourself. Mr. O'Grady, have

12

your other witnesses anything to testify in addition
to what Mrs. Hennesy has stated ?

"*Mr. O'Grady.*—I belave not, yer honer. The
material facts of the definse are sufficiently proven
by Misthress Hennesy's evidence. Av the Coort
plase, I have a few words to say in behalf of me
clients here, which, av the Coort will hear me, I will
make brief and to the point.

"*Judye.*—Go on.

"*Mr. O'Grady.*—Thin, av the Coort plase, I will
state that the ground of my definse of these gintlemen and ladies against the unfounded chairge of
their disturbin' the public pace, is that the chairge
is unthrue in point of fact. Sir, what are the facts?
A man dies, and his friends congregate about the
corpse to perform their last friendly offices to his
remains, in accordance with a custom justified by
thradition, ratified by usage, sanctified by antiquity,
vilified by these officers of the law when they call it
a disturbance of the public quiet, crucified when
they burst in the house of mournin' and interfered
wid it in the name of the law ; and, sir, I shall now
proceed to establish a definse, *bone fide*, with the
soundness of which I belave yer honor will be satisfied. Sir, the Constitution guarantees to my clients
freedom of conscience ; the stairs and sthripes wave

proudly over a land in which religious despotism never dare show its repulsive form; and yet these officers dare to say that a custom, which is almost a pairt of the religion of these my clients, is a disturbance of the public pace. Sir, the institutions of our counthry air endangered by such perceedin's. And who was they disturbin'? Wasn't every man and woman and child in Pacific Place of the same nationality of these my clients? Air not their ethnological instincts runnin' in the same channels? Was they disturbed? No! Every man and woman and child there would have admired the devotion of these my clients, to their ancient national thraditions and customs. There they was wan wid another doin' their last friendly offices to their deceased friend in a fraternal fight over his corpse. Sir, what a sublime spectacle for the human mind to contemplate. I wondher that the officers were not thransfixed by the solemnity and moral grandeur of the scene.

"*Judge.*—Mr. O'Grady, I think that the fact of the dead having come to life, and having been put to bed dead drunk, proves disastrous for your argument, even admitting its soundness.

"*Mr. O'Grady.*—Thrue it is, yer honor, that the wake was perceedin' without the corpse, as thradition has it, that wonst upon a time Hamlet was played widout the Prince of Denmark; but, yer honor, it was the fault of the corpse, and not of that assembly of mourners. If Timothy Garretty had chosen to have remained a dacintly-behaved corpse, thin the objection which yer honor has raised could not have weighed against me clients here, and I press it now upon yer honor should my clients here be held accountable for the shortcomings of the corpse? I think not, sir.

"*Judge.*—I think, Mr. O'Grady, you may dispense with further argument, as it would be superfluous. Mrs. Hennesy's house and its inmates have never been complained of before that I am aware of, and in consideration of this fact I'll discharge the prisoners, giving them warning, however, in the future that if they are any of them brought before me again, I shall not deal with them so leniently. You may go.

" The interesting party left the court.

" The business of the court having been quite extended, the Judge cast eyes upon the clock, observing that the hour was already advanced, but as he looked at the list of cases before him, he observed with a seeming satisfaction, that he had now reached the last; he felicitated himself with the idea that in a few moments he would be at liberty to leave the premises, and after finding his way to some neighboring restaurant, partake of his judicial sirloin steak and coffee. He was evidently fatigued, but he put on a good-humored face as he called out:

" 'Timothy Mulrooney.'

" 'Here, sir,' said a young Milesian, remarkable for nothing in particular; 'here I am, sir:' and Timothy Mulrooney stepped forward to the bar.

The Judge addressed the prisoner:

" 'Timothy,' said he, 'you are charged with disorderly conduct.'

" 'Yes sir, he is, and it's me that chairges him wid that same,' spoke up an old woman, dressed in a heavy, blue cloth cloak, and an antiquated cap and bonnet.

"*Judge.*—Are you the witness?

" *Woman.*—Av coorse I am, your honor, and it's me pride that I can spake against Tim Mulrooney—the dirty tief of the world that he is (to the prisoner), and I wondher, Tim, that you're not ashamed to howld up yer head before his honor.

"*Judge.*—Madame, state the facts as they occurred.

" *Witness.*—Well, plase your honor, it was on Friday mornin' or Saturday mornin', I don't know which; but be that as it may, it doesn't make anny difference, because it's about what followed that yer honor wants for to know, when I heard the horn of a fish-cairt in front of my door; sez I to myself, now Michael has come wid the porgies, and—

"*Judge.*—Who is Michael?

"*Witness.*—And don't ye know Michael, sure? he is my own child, and a betther-behaved and more dacent boy nor him never sang at a wake; and he can rade and write yer honor, as well as annybody, barrin' that whin he comes to the big words he has to skip them, and guess at what they mane; but that is not his fault, yer honor, for Michael never had any time to go to school, still—

"*Judge.*—Madame, you shouldn't let your tongue fly off in a tangent in this way. What we desire to know is relative to the charge preferred by you against Timothy Mulrooney, here.

"*Witness.*—Yes, your worship, I was just comin' to it when ye interrupted me. (To the prisoner)— Ah, you murdhering tief, it's on Blackwell's Island that ye ought to be, instead of bein' here to face his honor in the indacent way that ye'r doing now. (To the Judge)—Well, your honor, it was on Friday mornin' or Saturday mornin', I can't tell which, but be that as it may, it does not make anny difference, because it's about what followed that yer honor wants for to know, when I heard the horn of a fish-cairt in front of me door. Sez I to myself, Michael has come wid the porgies. You see, your honor, Michael owns a fish-cairt, and he sells fish, and what he doesn't sell he brings home for us to ate. He towld me in the morning, that he would thry for to save some of the porgies for dinner. Thin I wint out ov the door, and sure enough it was Michael. 'Michael,' sez I; 'What,' sez he; 'Is it here ye's air?' sez I; 'Sure it is,' sez he; 'Did you save the porgies?' sez I; 'Av coorse I did,' sez he; and wid that he commenced takin' out the fish from the cairt.

"*Judge.*—What has all this to do with Timothy Mulrooney's offensive conduct? you have not shown as yet that he has done anything wrong.

" *Witness.*—Yer honor need have no fears but I'll convince yez that a dirtier spalpeen nor him niver was allowed to go unhung among a dacent people. (To the prisoner)—Ah, Tim, ye villain, I wondher that the ship didn't sink wid ye on board when ye left the ould counthry; I'd like to see ye show a receipt wid yer passage-money paid, ye—

"*Judge.*—Madam, I must insist upon your address-ing yourself to the Court; you have no business to speak to the prisoner at all. Although he may have done wrong, yet so long as he is in my presence he shall be protected from the assaults of your tongue.

" *Witness* (excited).—The assaults of me tongue ! Howly St. Pathrick, do ye hear that? Yer honor, I'm a dacint woman wid a family of childher and divil a word was ever spoke against me charackther before.

"*Judge.*—I said nothing against your character. I want you to confine yourself to what Timothy Mulrooney did to disturb the peace and quiet of your domicile.

" *Witness.*—I will yer honor. It was on Friday mornin', or Saturday mornin', I don't know which, but be that as it may, it don't make anny difference, because it's about what followed that yer honor wants for to know ; ah, yer honor, I have it now—it was Friday mornin'—we was to have porgies for dinner, and not mate, because it was Friday—

"*Judge.*—All this is worse than nothing ; you are taking up the time of the court by your tedious talk, which, so far as I can see, has no bearing whatever on the charge you have seen fit to make against this man Timothy.

" *Witness.*—Haven't I been trying for the last ten minutes to tell ye, and ye'll not not let me? It's wid a bad grace that yer honor reproves me for not tellin' ye what I know, whin it's yerself that is interruptin' me. Well, yer honer, it was on Friday morning, whin I heard the horn of a fish-cairt in front of my door, sez I to myself, now Michael—

"*Judge.*—I don't want to hear that story any more. You have told that several times already. State the facts about Timothy. Come down to the time when he commences to figure.

"*Witness.*—Ah, bad luck to the thratement that I get here. Has any of my illusthrious family the O'Briens ever done annything against yer honer that yez should illthrait me in this way?

"*Judge.*—Not that I am aware of. Now go on with your evidence.

"*Witness.*—Well, yer honor, as I was about to tell ye, it was on Friday mornin' whin I heard the horn of a fish-cairt in front of my door. Sez I to myself —now Michael has come wid the porgies.

"*Judge* (impatiently).—Mrs. O'Brien, I—

"*Witness.*—Me name's not O'Brien; I'm a married woman, and me name is Flaherty; me name was O'Brien when I was a girl.

"*Judge.*—Well, then, Mrs. Flaherty, O'Brien, or whatever your name is, I have heard of these porgies and that fish-cart so often that they have grown stale;
12*

now tell me what occurred between you and Timothy Mulrooney?

"*Witness.*—How do I know but ye'll intherrupt me again before I have said five words?

"*Judge.*—You may rest assured that I will not if you will tell what Tim Mulrooney has done that is contrary to law.

"*Witness.*—I could tell ye enough to hang him a half-dozen times, if he had as manny necks as that; (to the prisoner) ye know I could, Tim, ye—

"*Judge* (perspiringly).—Mrs. O'Flaherty—

"*Witness.*—Flaherty, widout the O, yer honor.

"*Judge.*—Well, whatever your name is, you must not say anything to the prisoner in this court. Go on now, and if you will tell what he has done I'll not interrupt you.

"*Witness.*—Now remember yer promise, ye honor. It was on Friday mornin'—

"*Judge* (despairingly).—You're at it again. I—

"*Witness.*—Howly mother of Moses! I told yer honor how it would be wid ye; here I haven't said more nor five words before yer at yer owld thricks again.

"*Judge* (much vexed).—What did Timothy do with your fish?

"*Witness.*—He didn't do annything wid them that

time, barrin' that he saw Michael bring them in the house, and I heard him tell Biddy Mulrooney, his mother, who lives in the next room to me, that he would rather live on praties and bread, as they was a doin', than to ate stinkin' porgies that nobody else would buy; I know the Mulrooneys was jealous.

"*Judge.*—Did Timothy create any disturbance then?

"*Witness.*—No, yer honor, he didn't.

"*Judge.*—Then why did you have him arrested?

"*Witness.*—It was afther thin that the spalpeen made the disturbance.

"*Judge.*—When was that?

"*Witness.*—It was yestherday mornin'.

"*Judge.*—What did Timothy do?

"*Witness.*—It wasn't Tim, but his cat.

"*Judge.*—Then it seems that you have entered a charge against Timothy Mulroony of disorderly conduct, which, by right, you should have made against Timothy Mulrooney's cat, always provided that cats are amenable to municipal law.

"*Witness.*—By my sowl, yer honor, ye've got it mixed up again. Now why didn't ye wait until I could tell ye.

"*Judge.*—Go on; I am reconciled to my fate. As

a particular favor, I should like to have you finish within a half hour.

"*Witness*.—Well, yer honor, as I was tellin' ye, the Mulrooneys was jealous of us because we had fish and they didn't. Yestherday mornin' Michael brought home more porgies (the Judge here heaved a deep sigh) and I laid them on top of a barrel in the passage to wait till I could dress them; what next, yer honor, did I see but Tim Mulrooney's big tom cat on the barrel atin' the fish; I heaved a pratie at the cat and it ran off wid the porgies; just thin I saw Tim Mulrooney laughing at what the cat was doin'; I know the blackgaird had towld the cat to ate the porgies; I called to Michael, and I run toward Tim to bate the tief as he deserved, whin my foot slipped and I furled over on the broad of my back; wid that Tim laughed the more, and Michael run to him, and was about to give him a tap on the sconce, whin Tim struck Michael a blow in his bowels, which quite prostrated him on the floor; with that I ran and got the M. P., who brought the murderin' tief to the station-house.

"*Judge*.—Well, Mrs. Flaherty, I think, according to your own story, the prisoner acted more in his own defence than any other way.

"*Witness.*—In his own definse! Bad luck to the tongue that says so. Is ——

"*Judge* (to prisoner).—Timothy Mulrooney, I am by no means sure that your cat did not eat the Flahertys' fish with your connivance. If the cat did so, you did wrong; but for that you are sufficiently punished by your imprisonment last night. I think you might have been less hasty in striking Michael. Is Michael in court?

"*Mrs. Flaherty.*—He is. Stand up, Michael, before his honor.

" Mrs. Flaherty, Michael and Timothy were standing together in a row.

"*Judge.*—Now I am going to insure perfect harmony in your house for six months to come; I shall bind each of you over in the sum of $200 to keep the peace.

"This was almost too great a humiliation for the blood of the O'Briens to bear; but there was no alternative. Mrs. O'Brien Flaherty satisfied herself as well as she could by looking screw-drivers at the Judge; Michael appeared demure, and Timothy appeared jolly. The bonds were given, and the interesting trio left the court.

"The Judge rose from his chair, and made a bee line for breakfast."

During the various narrations which were given during the evening, Mr. Quackenbush remained seated in the corner, saying nothing and doing as much. His eyes were partially closed, and an occasional sigh was all that escaped him.

When Mr. Dropper concluded the reading of his contributions, it was moved that Mr. Quackenbush open his mouth, and say something, under the penalty of having it pried open with the poker.

This caused Mr. Quackenbush to open his eyes; and, after various preliminary hems and coughs, he announced that there was a certain rule of evidence which gave a witness the right to refuse to say anything tending to criminate himself. He should avail himself of that rule. Having said these words, Mr. Quackenbush rolled over on the floor, drew himself into double bow knot, and was soon snoring against noise.

In the meantime Mr. Spout had taken the floor, and stated that he had on one occasion been over at the Essex Market Police Court. He was there the involuntary witness of the trial of a case, which might account for the non-communicative disposition manifested on the present occasion by Mr. Quackenbush. During the proceedings, the justice called out the name of R. Percy De Lancy Blobb; and in response to the call a tall individual arose and came forward. "I thought I recognized in the individual in question," continued Mr. Spout, "a person whom I had seen before, and I was not mistaken. He was wild, and disposed to regale the assembled company with a numerous collection of songs, which he had at his tongue's end. His dress was much disarranged.

"The evidence of the officer who had arrested the tall gentleman, went to show that he had offended against the laws, by disturbing the rest and quiet of an unappreciative neighborhood, by bawling forth at midnight most unmelodious yells, which, when he was apprehended, he assured the officer were capital imitations of Sontag, Grisi, and Grisi's new baby. When arrested the individual was in a plebeian state of drunkenness—not so much so but that he could sing, as he called it, and could talk after an original fashion of his own. His ideas were slightly confused; he informed the officer that he had been to hear Louisa Crown sing the Pyne Diamonds, and that he met a friend who took him to a billiard shop to see a clam race; that he and his friend bet the whisky on the result; that he drunk for both, and that they had passed the remainder of the evening in a 'magnorious manner,' singing 'Storm Columbus,' 'Yankee Boodles,' and the 'Scar Strangled Bladder.'

"The officer had taken him to the lock-up, where he had finished the night singing 'Good Old Daniel,' whistling the 'Prima Donna Waltz,' and playing an imaginary piano-solo on the floor, in which attempt he had worn off some of his finger-nails. When he was before the court he had not yet recovered his normal condition. He was still musically obstinate, and refused to answer any questions of the Judge, or make any remarks, except in scraps of songs, which he sang in a low voice, mixing up the tunes in a most perplexing manner. Being possessed of an excellent memory, and having a large assortment of melodies at his command, his answers were sometimes more amusing than relevant. The Judge proceeded to interrogate him somewhat as follows :—

"*Judge.*—What is your name, sir?

"*Prisoner.*—'My name is Robert Kidd, as I sailed '—

"*Indignant Officer.*—He lies, your honor. Last night he said his name was Blobb.

"*Judge.*—Where do you live?

"*Prisoner.*—'Erin, Erin is my home.'

"*Knowing Officer.*—He isn't an Irishman, Judge;

he's a Connecticut Yankee, and lives in East Broadway.

"*Prisoner.*—'That's eight times to-day you have kissed me before.'

"*Officer.*—Please, your honor, he's an octagonal liar, I didn't.

"*Judge.*—Where did you get your liquor?

"*Prisoner.*—'Way down south in Cedar street; rinctum'—

"*Judge* (to officer).—What's that he says?

"*Attentive Officer.*—At Ringtown's in Cedar street.

"*Judge.*—What number in Cedar street?

"*Prisoner.*—'Forty horses in the stable.'

"*Officious Officer.*—Ringtown's, No. 40 Cedar street, your honor.

"*Prisoner.*—(Voluntary remark, sotto voce.) 'A jay bird sat on a hickory limb—he winked at me and I winked at him.'

"*Indignant Officer.*—Who're you winkin' at?

"*Prisoner.*—'Nelly Bly, shuts her eye.'

"*Officer.*—You'd better shut your mouth.

"*Judge.*—What have you got to say, prisoner?

"*Prisoner.*—'Hear me, Norma.'

"*Officer.*—Well, go on, go on.

"*Prisoner.*—'O blame not the bard.'

"*Judge.*—Nobody to blame but yourself.

"*Prisoner.*—' Did you ever hear tell of Kate Kearney ?'

"*Knowing Officer.*—Keeps a place in Mott street, your honor.

"*Prisoner.*—' O ! O ! O ! O ! O ! Sally is the gal for me.'

"*Judge* (to officer).—Who is Sally ? Some disreputable female I suppose.

"*Officer.*—She went up to the Island to-day, sir.

"*Prisoner.*—' O tell me, where is Fancy bred.'

"*Judge.*—I don't know anything about your fancy bread, if you have anything to say, go on.

"*Prisoner.*—' We'll all go bobbing around.'

" The Judge here became indignant, and demanded if he had a friend to become bail for him, to which query the prisoner hiccuped out,

" ' I'll never, never find—a better friend than old dog Tray.'

"*Judge.*—Can't take him, he is not responsible.

"*Prisoner.*—' I give thee all, I can no more.'

"*Judge.*—It won't do, sir, I shall fine you $10.

"*Prisoner.*—' That's the way the money goes— pop goes the weasel.'

"*Indignant Officer.*—I'll pop you over the head presently.

"*Prisoner.*—'There's whisky in the jug.'

"*Officer.*—You'll be there, too, shortly.

"*Judge.*—If you can't pay you must go to jail.

"*Prisoner.*—'Give me a cot in the valley I love.'

"*Judge.*—Very well, sir, I'll do it. Tombs, ten days.

"*Prisoner.*—'I dreamt that I dwelt in marble halls.'

"The officer was about removing the individual below, when I came to the rescue, and informed the Judge that the prisoner was a friend of mine, that this was the first occasion in which he had ever manifested such eccentricities, and if he would let him off from the punishment this time, I would take him to his home and see that he never disturbed the city by his yells in the future.

"The prisoner turned his eyes upon me, and again broke out:

"'Good news from home, good news for me'——

"'Mr. Blobb,' said the Judge, 'if I let you off this time, will you cease going on these drunken sprees?'

"*Prisoner.*—'I'll touch not, taste not, handle not, whate'er intoxicates.'

"*Judge.*—I hope that when we meet again it will be under more favorable auspices to yourself——

"*Prisoner* (interrupting).—'Meet me by moonlight alone, and I will tell thee.'

"*Judge* (resuming).—For you're in a bad plight now to appear among the ladies.

"*Prisoner.*—'Oh! I'm the boy for bewitching them.'

"*Judge.*—Not when you're drunk, I imagine.

"*Prisoner.*—'A man's a man, for a' o' that.'

"*Judge.*—You may go, sir. Good day.

"*Prisoner.*—'Oh, give to me that better word that comes from the heart, Good bye.'

"I managed to get my friend, Mr. Blobb, out of the court-room, and subsequently, with some difficulty, I succeeded in putting him to bed in my apartment, where I kept him for twenty-four hours, until he had recovered from his temporary aberration. He has since that time been in a normal state, except that he appears melancholy at times. He is well enough, however,——

"To be here this evening," said Quackenbush, interrupting; "for know ye that Mr. R. Percy Delancy Blobb is now before you in the person of myself, and I am here to-night to ask forgiveness,

which, if you don't give to me, I shall take immediate measures to expel you all from the club."

It was immediately voted that Mr. Quackenbush
be forgiven, on condition that he would disclose the
facts which led to his being found a prisoner in the
Essex Market Police Court.

This, Mr. Quackenbush said he would do and do
it now, and after finding room for a glass of ginger-
wine, proceeded to narrate his experience.

He stated, substantially, that the whole difficulty
grew out of a love affair. He had become deeply
infatuated with an unknown and beautiful blonde.
He had often met her in the street, in theatres, and
concert-rooms, and his intense admiration ripened
into a deep love. He was unable to learn who she
was until a fortnight previously, when he found a
friend who was well acquainted with her, and who
undertook to bring about an introduction. Things
wore a brighter aspect then. The sun was more
brilliant; the moon shed a less melancholy light;
lager bier tasted better; oysters appeared fatter;
peanuts seemed always roasted just enough, and, in
fact, he felt quite satisfied with life, and the world
generally, and resolved to postpone indefinitely a
purpose he had entertained of buying three cents'
worth of arsenic. But a day or two before the scene

in the Police Court in which he figured, he found
himself in a stage, and directly opposite was the
identical object of his admiration and affection. He
hitched from one side on his seat to the other; put
one leg on the other, and then reversed them;
looked out of the window, and then at her; scratched
his ears; pulled up his collar; brushed the dust
from his pantaloons; put his hands in his pockets;
pulled them out, and did many ridiculous things
which he would not have done had she not been
present. She stopped the stage on one of the
avenues, and handed him a five-franc piece to pay
the driver. The driver, as usual, gave change in
small pieces. He counted it to see that it was all
right; found it to be so, and informed her of the
fact. The streets being very muddy, he resolved to do
the genteel in the way of assisting her out of the
vehicle; made his exit; put one foot six inches into
a mud-hole, and the other on the edge of the curb-
stone; lifted the lady to the side-walk in safety, at the
expense of bursting off two suspender-buttons, and
his vest-buckle, a slip down causing his nose to fall
against the tire, his knees into the mud, his shoulder
against the stage-steps, and caving in his hat. But
all this didn't trouble him in the least, as he expected
to be more than remunerated by an approving smile

on the part of the lady. He turned his face towards her, and found her engaged in counting the change, which he had pronounced to be all right, as if she suspected that he would be guilty of cheating her out of a stray sixpence, and thus hazard his chances for salvation. The effect of the disappointment, on him, was frightful. He felt a sickening sensation; stopped at the nearest whisky-shop, and imbibed; went to another, and took a nip; proceeded to a third, and smiled; reached a fourth, and took a horn; entered a fifth, and drank, and so on, *ad libitum*. At last he reached Niblo's; saw a flaming poster announcing that Louisa Pyne was to sing in the "Crown Diamonds;" bought a ticket; took several drinks and a seat. His ears had become unusually critical. Thought he could beat Harrison singing, and to satisfy himself, he rose up, and commenced to slaughter a peice, which Harrison had just executed. There was an evident want of appreciation of his abilities, for he was hustled out in double-quick time. He then went to a bar-room, and called for something to drink, which deliberate act was the last circumstance he remembered, previous to recognizing Mr. Spout in his room in the afternoon of the following day, when he inquired of that gentleman if he wouldn't be so kind as to prevent the nigger boy from striking him on the head with a poker, as he thought he had done it long enough.

A vote of forgiveness to Mr. Quackenbush was carried, after which the entire club went to sleep.

"The Hamlet Fight."

"Murder most foul, as in the best it is;
But this most foul, strange, and unnatural."

A few days after the events recorded in the last chapter, a new trick was invented to obtain under, false pretences, the money of the public. A number of needy and seedy individuals having been told that in England several of the most dis-

13

289

tinguished literary men in that country had given a few theatrical exhibitions with great success, conceived the plan of exhibiting, in a similar manner, in the city of New York, a number of authors, artists and other celebrities, admitting the public at twenty-five cents per head. That it might look less like a humbug, and by way of hiding, as far as possible, the swindle which was only too transparent, after all, it was announced that the living poets and painters would be shown all alive in secure cages, undergoing a periodical stirring-up by the keeper, and being benevolently fed in the presence of the spectators afterward.

Preparations had been made to secure the services of the biggest authors, the most notorious painters, the largest sized sculptors, the most melodious poets, and the most sanguinary editors the country could produce. The anxious world expected nothing less than to see the author of " Thanatopsis " appear as *Hamlet* in black-tights and a slouched hat—and he who invented " Evangeline " and "Hiawatha " come on as the *Ghost* with a pasteboard helmet and a horse-hair beard. Who should be *Laertes* but he who "skulped" the Greek Slave, or what editor could play " the king " like the democratic conductor of the *Tribune ?* who, in assuming the crown, was

to doff the white hat, " positively for one night only ?"
The *Queen of Denmark* would of course be represented by the architect of "Uncle Tom's Cabin,"
whose familiarity with courts and royalty would enable her to invest the character with life-like interest.
The public had made up its mind to be content with
no *Ophelia* except Ruth Hall, for no one else
could play the crazy scenes so admirably. But
alas for the expectations of the misguided public—
the illustrious individuals aforesaid would not come,
and consequently the public were compelled to
witness the consummation of the dreadful tragedy,
by authors whose works they had never heard of ;
painters whose productions were unknown to the
world, and editors whom a close investigation resolved into obscure scribblers.

To this literary exhibition Overdale, Wagstaff,
and John Spout resolved to go—Overdale to give
the necessary explanations, Wagstaff to make a
transcript of his friend's valuable remarks, and John
Spout (himself an amateur artist) to see the cele-
brated men of his own profession, whose contributions to art had been so persistently kept out of
sight.

The performance was to take place in the Academy
of Music, a building designed and completed by a

diabolically ingenious architect, who endeavored to construct a theatre in such a manner that one half the audience could not hear, and the other half could not see, and who succeeded to admiration.

Our friends obtained seats in that part of the house where they could see, though it was not possible to *hear* a word.

After a great many preliminary flourishes and false starts by the members of the orchestra, they set off as nearly together as they could, in obedience to the frantic gestures of the leader, who flourished his fiddle-bow with as much energy and vindictiveness as if he had been insanely endeavoring to kill mosquitoes with it, in forty different directions at once.

Finally the curtain went up amid the uproarious applause of the assembled multitude, interrupted only by a small boy in the gallery, who hissed like a whole flock of enraged wild-geese, having been stationed there especially for the performance of this sibilant duty by an avenging washerwoman, to whom one of the amateurs owed four and sixpence; his dissenting voice was, however, soon hushed by the police, who put him out, and didn't give him his money back, after which the exhibition proceeded.

To give a full description of one half of the ridiculous performances indulged in by these deluded persons—to tell of the new readings which they gave, and the old readings which they didn't give—to relate how carefully they avoided the traps, and with what commendable caution they kept away from the footlights—to give an idea of the bedlamitish ingenuity they had displayed in the selection of wardrobe, how each one had put on the most inappropriate articles imaginable, and how they could not have been more incongruously attired if they had been all dressed in sheep's grey breeches and straw hats—to dilate upon the disasters which befell the said wardrobe, how the tunics caught in the wings, and the shoulder-cloaks got singed by the side-lights; how the ladies' trains were in everybody's way, and their feathers in everybody's eyes—how, in their confusion, when they painted their faces, they put the wrong colors in the wrong places, and some of them went on with white cheeks, chalked lips, and eyebrows colored a bright vermilion—how the gilt crowns got bent and battered until they looked like ancient milk-pans with the bottoms melted out—how the flannel ermine on the regal calico robes got greasy, and looked like tripe—how the wax pearls melted and the glass ones broke—how the " supes " painted their whiskers uneven, and got their wigs on wrong side before—how some of them couldn't get their armor on at all, but how one enterprising individual, having succeeded to his satisfaction, came on to deliver a message, with his sandals in his hand, his helmet on one foot, his breast-plate on the other, and his leg-pieces strapped on his shoulders—to tell how the *Ghost* got chilly and played the last scene in an overcoat, and proved that he was a substantial Native American Ghost, by making two extemporaneous speeches, in excellent English, to the audience—to do full justice to the miscellaneous assortment of *legs*, then and there congregated, and relate how some were bow-legs, and some were shingle-legs, some were broomstick-legs, some were wiry legs, and some were shoulder-of-mutton legs—to give an accurate relation of the various expedients resorted to, to remedy the most noticeable defects in those legs, and state that some were padded on the sides, and some at the ankles, and how, in not a few instances, the padding slipped away from its original position, thereby putting the calves on the shins, and causing the knees to resemble deformed india-rubber foot-balls—and to give a reliable history of the unheard-of antics indulged in by the said fantastic legs, after their symmetry had been perfected by the means just written—how some went crooked, some sideways, and some wouldn't go at all; how some minced with short steps, like a racking pony, and others stepped along as if they had seven-league boots on; how some moved with convulsive hitches, as if they were clockwork legs, and the springs were out of order; how some worked spasmodically up and down in the same place, and didn't get along at all, as if they were legs which had struck for higher wages; and how others dashed ahead, as if they did not intend to stop until they had transported their bewildered proprietors out of sight of the audience, as if they were machine legs, with the steam turned on, and weights on the safety-valve; how some went on the stage and wouldn't go off, and how others went off and wouldn't go on, until they were coaxed on by their agonized owners, a long time after the cue came—to tell how the red fire burned green, and the blue fire would not burn at all—how the call-boy got tipsy, and was not forthcoming—how the property-man fell over the sheet-iron thunder, and stuck his head into a pot of red paint, which made him look like a modern edition of Charles the First with his head cut off—how the grave-diggers got into the grave and couldn't get out—how *Hamlet* and *Laertes* could hardly get

in at all; and how, when they did get in, they made
the gravel fly—how the wrong men came on at the
wrong time, and how, as a general thing, the right
men didn't ever come on—how *Guildenstern* spoke
Ophelia's lines, how *Horatio* tried to speak one of
Hamlet's speeches, and danced a frantic hornpipe
with rage because he couldn't think how it began,
and how *Polonius* couldn't speak at all, and so
went home—how nobody could remember what
Shakspeare said, and so everybody said what Shakspeare didn't say, and hadn't said, and wouldn't have
said, under any circumstances—how some of the
men swore, and some of the women wanted to, but
postponed it, and how the butchery proceeded, with
many mishaps and multitudinous mistakes, and how
the audience applauded, and cheered, and laughed at
the dismal tragedy, evidently considering it the live-
liest farce of the season, are facts, falsehoods, and
circumstances, both real and supposititious, which
could not be compressed within the limits of a single
volume.

Hamlet was personated by an aspiring youth,
whose physical dimensions were not up to the army
standard, and who couldn't have gathered fruit from
a currant-bush without high-heeled boots on; while
the lady who represented his mother would have

been compelled to stoop in order to pick pippins from the tallest apple-tree that ever grew. By the side of her illustrious son, she looked perfectly capable of taking him up in her arms, giving him his dinner after the usual maternal fashion, and afterwards disposing of him in the trundle-bed, to complete his infant slumbers.

Overdale explained that they had tried to get a bigger *Hamlet*, but that, upon the whole, he thought the little fellow would "speak his piece" pretty well, taking into consideration the fact, that in the dying groans, he was supposed to have no superior.

Wagstaff was totally ignorant of the plot, and as from ' the obfuscation of the performers, no one could have formed the slightest idea of what they were all talking about, he seemed in no very fair way to find out anything about it.

The peculiar rendition of the story of the King of Denmark was so uncertain, that even John Spout found it exceedingly difficult to tell where they were or how they would come out, or what they intended to do next. He was a little uncertain whether the queen would finally subdue *Hamlet*, or *Hamlet* succeed in thrashing the queen. In the closet scene, especially, the battle was conducted with such varying success that it was impossible to bet, with any

13*

kind of certainty, on the result, or to prognosticate, with reliability, whether *Hamlet* would knock his mother down with a chair, and damage her maternal countenance with the heels of his boots, or whether the old lady would succeed in *her* design, which was evidently to conquer her rebellious offspring, and give him a good spanking. Neither could he tell whether *Laertes* would kill *Horatio*, *Hamlet*, or the *Second Grave-digger*, who stood behind the wing, with his hands in his pockets, and his breeches in his boots. He was also a little undecided as to which was *Polonius*, and which was the king, and when the player queen came on, he thought it was only *Ophelia*, with a different-colored petticoat on. John swore the *Ghost* looked as if he hadn't had any dinner, and said he was perfectly certain his ghost-ship had been refreshing his invisible bowels with a mug of ale, behind the scenes, because when he came on the last time, with the broomstick in his hand, he could see the foam on his whiskers.

One of the richest and most incomprehensible scenes ever witnessed on the modern stage was the final one between *Hamlet* and the *Ghost*, who, finding the weather chilly, had done his best to mitigate his sufferings by putting on an overcoat. *Hamlet*, trying to look fierce, holding his sword at arm's length, performing a kind of original fancy-dance, as he followed the spiritual remains of his ghostly father across the stage—*Hamlet*, the mortal, being about the size of a mutton-ham, while his father, the immortal, supposed to be exceedingly ethereal, was tall enough and stout enough for a professional coal-heaver, instead of an amateur ghost—the intangible spirit, moreover, having one hand in his overcoat pocket, to keep his fingers warm, while in the other he flourished a short broomstick, as if to keep his degenerate scion at a respectful distance, were so ludicrous, that John Spout seized Wagstaff's book, and produced the sketch to be found at the beginning of this chapter.

And in the last death-scene *Hamlet* really won such honors as were never before accorded to mortal tragedian; being by this time a little doubtful whom to kill, he made an end of the entire company in rotation. First, he stabbed the *King*, who rolled over once or twice, and died with his legs so tangled up in the *Queen's* train that *she* had to expire in a hard knot; then he stabbed *Laertes*, who died cross-legged; then he stabbed *Osric;* and not content with this, he tripped up his heels and stood on his stomach, till he died in an agony of indigestion; then he tried to stick *Horatio*, but only succeeded in knocking his wig off; and then, turning up stage, made extensive preparations for terminating his own existence.

First, as everybody was dead, and everybody's legs were lying round loose, he had to lay them out of the way carefully, so as not to interfere with the comfort of the corpses; then he picked up all the swords and laid them cautiously in a corner, so that the points shouldn't stick in him when he fell; then he looked up at the curtain to see that he was clear of that, then he looked down at the traps to see that he was clear of them, and having at last arranged everything to his satisfaction, he proceeded to go systematically through his dying agonies, to the great satisfaction of the audience. Suffice it to say, that when the spasms were ended, and he had finally become a " cold corpus," his black tights were very dirty and had holes in the knees.

When the curtain went down *Hamlet* was too exhausted to get up, and instantly everybody rushed to the rescue; those he had slaughtered but a few minutes before, forgot their mortal wounds, and hastened to the murderer with something to drink. The *King* rushed up with a pewter mug of beer; *Horatio* presented the brandy-bottle; the *Ghost* handed him a glass of gin and sugar; the *Queen* gave him the little end of a Bologna sausage and a piece of cheese; the stage carpenter, in his bewilderment, could think of nothing but the glue-pot; the property man hastened to his aid with a tin cup full of rose-pink, and a plate-full of property apple-dumplings (ingeniously but deceptively constructed out of canvas and bran), while an insane scene-shifter first deluged him with water, and then offered him the bucket to dry himself with.

John Spout, who had been behind the curtain, and witnessed this last performance, immediately came out, borrowed Wagstaff's note-book, and left therein his pictorial reminiscence of this scene as follows:

Overdale had been profuse in his explanations of

the many curious scenes, and Wagstaff had noted down his words carefully in his memorandum-book Once when the *Ghost* tripped and fell through the scenery, caving in the side of a brick house, and kicking his spiritual heels through the belfry of a church in the background, Overdale said that this was *Ophelia*, who had been taken suddenly crazy, and in her frenzy had imagined it necessary to hasten to the nearest grocery for a bar of soap to saw her leg off with. *Polonius*, he explained, was *Horatio*, and *Hamlet* was a little boy who run on errands for the cook of the palace, by which culinary appellation he designated the Queen of Denmark. He said the plot of the piece was, that the king wanted to marry the cook, but her relatives objected to the alliance, because his majesty hadn't got shirts enough for a change.

All of which was carefully written down by Wagstaff, with divers alterations, emendations, additions, and extemporaneous illustrations, by John Spout.

This last-named individual asserts to the present time that he cannot tell who were the most humbugged—the people who paid their money, and laughed at the play under the impression that it was a farce, or the unfortunates who performed the play, laboring under the hallucination that they were act-ing tragedy.

All were, however, satisfied, that it was a kink of the Elephant's tail, which he has not yet uncurled in any city of America—save Gotham.

Mrs. Throughby Daylight's Fancy Dress Jam.

"Black spirits and white,
Red spirits and grey,
Mingle, mingle "——

r. REMINGTON DROPPER had a great respect for upper tendom; was almost inclined to admit, without question, its claims to the worship of the vulgar masses, and confessed that when he saw one whom he took to be a leader of fashion coming, he felt an involuntary movement of his right hand towards his hat. He admitted that he had, by this manner of doing indiscriminate homage to well-dressed people, on several occasions taken off

804

his hat to notorious horse-jockeys, faro-dealers, and gamblers.

"However," said John Spout, "if you want to go to a grand fancy dress ball, where you will meet all 'the world,' as these try-to-be-fashionable people call those who have scraped together dollars enough to entitle them to their royal notice, I can very easily get you an invitation. Mrs. Throughby Daylight, whose husband made a fortune by selling patent medicine, and thereby purged himself of poverty and plebeianism together, gives, in a short time, a grand fantasquerade, which is intended to be the most consolidated fancy dress jam of the season. Do you want to go?"

"Go," replied Dropper, "how can I go? I don't know Mrs. Throughby Daylight, or Mr. Throughby Daylight, or any of the Daylights, so that Daylight is all moonshine."

"Dropper," was the response, "you're young; I excuse that, for you can't help it; but you're also *green*, which I cannot forgive; your verdancy is particularly noticeable when you revive the absolute absurdity of supposing that it is necessary to be acquainted with a lady before you are invited to attend her parties. That antiquated idea has been long since exploded. Why, my dear sir, it is no more necessary that you should have ever previously heard of a woman whose 'jam' you receive an invitation to attend, than it is probable she knows who *you* are, or where the devil you come from.

Dropper was bewildered.

"It is a positive fact," continued Spout. "Why, bless your innocent eyes, a woman of fashion no more knows the names of the individuals who attend her grand party, than she knows who took tea last night with the man in the moon. She merely orders music and provisions, makes out a list of a few persons she *must* have, has her rooms actually measured, allows eight inches square to a guest; thus having estimated the number that can crowd into her house, she multiplies it by two, which gives the amount of invitations to be issued, after which she leaves the rest to Brown. Brown takes the list; Brown finds the required number of guests. Brown invites whom he pleases; Brown fills the house with people, and Brown, and only Brown, knows who they are, where they came from, or how the deuce they got their invitations."

Dropper, still more bewildered, inquired who Brown was.

"Brown," explained John Spout, "is the Magnus Apollo of fashionable society—he is the sexton of

Graceless Chapel, and no one can be decently married, or fashionably buried without his assistance. He has a wedding face and a funeral face, but never forgets himself and cries over the bride or laughs at the mourners; he is great as a sexton, but it is only in his character of master of ceremonies at a party, that he rises into positive sublimity—he is the consoler of aspiring unfashionables, who have got plenty of money, and want to cut a swell, but don't know how to begin. He is the furnisher of raw material on short notice, for fashionable parties of all dimensions; his genius is equal to any emergency, though, as the latest fashion is to invite three times as many people as can get into the house at any one time, Brown is often put to his trumps. Mrs. Codde Fishe last week wanted to give a party, and, of course, called on Brown. Brown measured the parlors; they would only hold 1728, even by putting the chairs down cellar, and turning the piano up endways. Mrs. Codde Fishe was in despair. Mrs. P. Nutt had received 1800 at her party the night before, and if she couldn't have 2000 she would be ruined. Brown's genius saved her. 'Mrs. F.,' said he, 'though we must invite 2000 people, and though we must have 2000 people in the house, they need not be all there at one time, and they need not all stay.'

" 'Certainly not,' said Mrs. Fishe.

" 'I'll manage it,' said the indefatigable Brown—and Brown did manage it. He got 272 retail dry-goods clerks, whom there didn't anybody know, dressed them in white gloves and the required fixens, so they looked almost as well as men. Well, sir, if you'll believe it, Brown had his 272 clerks arrive at the door, eleven at a time, in hired hack-ney-coaches, announced them, by high-flown names, to the hostess, had them march in single file through the parlors to the back door, where he had a man waiting to conduct them over the garden-fence by a step-ladder, and so get them out of the way to make room for more.

"Mrs. Lassiz Candee had but 1439 names on her list; she wanted 1800. Brown was summoned. Brown heard the trouble. Brown produced from his pocket a list of names twenty-one yards in length. For a moderate compensation he furnished Mrs. Candee with a yard and a half of literary celebrities, three yards of 'Shanghaes,' five yards and a quarter of polka dancers, and about fourteen feet of foreign-ers, with beards and moustaches for show-pieces, and to give the thing a 'researcha' look.

"But, not to be too tiresome, Dropper, I am on Brown's list of eligibles, and can get your name added, also."

Remington eagerly accepted the offer, and three days after they found on their table two huge envelopes, addressed respectively to "Mr. John Spout," and "Mr. Remington Dropper." Remington, trembling with haste, broke open his at once, and discovered a card about the size of a washboard, on which was a communication to the effect that Mrs. Throughby Daylight requested the pleasure of the company of Mr. Remington Dropper, and that it was to be a fancy dress party, and he was requested to appear in costume, all of which he only discovered by calling John Spout to his assistance, who condescendingly explained everything.

Remington was overjoyed, but in answer to all his anxious inquiries concerning the manner of procuring the invitation, he only elicited from John Spout the mysterious monosyllable, BROWN!

"What does it mean by coming 'in *costume?*' How am I to dress? What shall I put on, and where shall I get it?" inquired he.

John explained. "It means that you are to disguise yourself in an un-Christian attire of some description, making yourself look as unlike a 'human gentleman' as possible—call yourself a 'Gondolier,' a 'Brigand,' a 'Minstrel Boy,' or some other sentimental or romantic name, and cut as big a splurge in your borrowed clothes as possible. If you know anybody who belongs to the theatre, you can easily borrow a rig; if not, you'll have to hire it of a Jew, and give security that you'll bring it back."

For four days Mr. Dropper was in a state of feverish undecision respecting his choice of a character. At the end of that time he was still wavering between a "Turk," a "Monk," and "Jack Sheppard." By John Spout's suggestion he resolved to decide the matter by a throw of the dice, which method made a "Turk" of him for the eventful evening, the "Monk" getting deuce, ace, and a five, "Jack Sheppard" scoring but eleven, while his oriental highness came off victorious, by means of two fours and a six. John Spout was going as a Choctaw Indian, so that he could smoke all the time and no one would find fault and say that he was vulgar.

The wished-for evening arrived, and Remington began to dress at four in the afternoon, so as to be in time. By the assistance of two Irishmen and a black boy he got his dress on at half-past six; and at a quarter to seven he sunk exhausted into a arm-chair, and went to sleep.

John's own toilette was quickly made; he had borrowed his dress from a friend, who attended in person to put it on for him.

When they were ready, the black boy was dispatched for a hack, into which they both got; after experiencing some difficulty from Spout's war club, which got tangled in Remington's trousers, and being a good deal exasperated by Dropper's scimitar which *would* get between John Spout's legs and interfere with his breech cloth.

At last they approximated the house, and their carriage took its place in the rear of a long line which had formed in front of Mrs. Throughby Daylight's mansion, and anxiously waited for those in front to move out of the way, and give them a chance to get out.

They could hear in the distance the shrill whistle and the voice of the indefatigable Brown, shouting "Room for Mrs. Rosewood's carriage;" "Clear the way for Mrs. Fizgiggle's vehicle;" "Let Mrs. Funk's establishment come up;" and then Brown would disappear into the house, and a faint echo of Brown would be heard from the inside, announcing these visitors as "Mrs. Noseblood," Mrs. Buzfiggle," and "Mrs. Junk," it being a peculiarity of Brown, that although he might get the names of the guests right the first time, he never announced them at the door without some ludicrous perversion.

Our friends at length attained the entrance, and,

having been interrogated by Brown as to who they were, and having told him " a Turk " and " a Choctaw," they were instantly ushered by that individual into the presence of the versicolored crowd, and announced, in a voice of thunder, as " Mr. Squirt " and " Mr. Bucksaw."

As they had come in a carriage and were prepared for immediate conquest, they had no overcoats or hats to dispose of, and were consequently ushered directly into the first of the three parlors, they held a consultation as to which was the hostess ; and what the least perilous manner of getting at her, concluded that it was not necessary for a Turk or a Heathen to be so particular about the rules of Christian society, and so they dispensed with the usual entering salute.

Remington Dropper soon found that he was not the only oriental in the room ; there were four other Turks, and a great many Moguls, so that he only made up the half dozen, but he consoled himself with the reflection that his turban was the biggest, and that the toes of his slippers turned up higher than any of the rest.

But beside the "malignant and the turbaned Turks," there was a great variety of other unexpected characters on exhibition in Mrs. Daylight's apartments—kings, queens, gipsies, and highway-

men, milkmaids, who not only couldn't milk, but
probably couldn't tell a cow from a cod-fish, pea-
sant-girls with jewelry enough on for princesses, and
princesses with red faces and feet big enough for
peasants, tambourine girls begging for pennies which
they couldn't get, and bouquet girls trying to sell
flowers from a large assortment, consisting of two
geranium leaves and a rose-bud, French grisettes,
who couldn't speak French, and Spanish noblemen,
who talked most unmistakable down-east Yankee,
Highlanders with pasteboard shields and bare knees,
army officers who didn't know how to shoulder arms,
sailors who couldn't tell the keel from the jib-boom,

14

or swear positively that the tiller wasn't the long-
boat, the Queen of Sheba in gold spectacles, robbers,
brigands, freebooters, corsairs, bandits, pirates, buc-
caneers, highwaymen, fillibusters, and smugglers in
such quantities, that it might be supposed that our
best society is two-thirds made up of these amiable
persons.   There were three Paul Prys, four Irishmen, and thirteen Yankees, equipped with jackknives
and shingles, seven Hamlets, and fourteen Ophelias,
one Lear, two Richards, and five Shylocks, eight
Macbeths, three Fitz James, and half a dozen Rob
Roys, who made a very respectable assortment of
Scotchmen; there were also twenty-one monks, quite
a regiment; this *was* considered strange, but the next
day, when most of the silver was missing, it was
immediately surmised that these reverend gentlemen
were thieves, who had obtained surreptitious admission, and carried off the valuables under their priestly
robes.

There were also a few ladies, particular friends of
the hostess, who appeared, by permission, in no costume more ridiculous than that which they were
accustomed to wear daily, but who displayed the
usual amount of whalebone developments.

After the band arrived and was stationed in the
conservatory out of sight, an attempt was made to get

up a dance. Spout introduced Dropper to a princess of his acquaintance, and Dropper, as in duty bound, asked her to waltz, and actually proceeded to carry out his intention.

As some sixty other couples attempted the same feat at the same time, and as there wasn't room for any one man to dance without stepping on the heels of his neighbor, the scene instantly assumed a peculiar appearance. Dropper first whisked his partner against a flower girl and upset her basket, then against a Paul Pry, and demolished his horn spectacles, then he tumbled her into the stomach of a Falstaff and rolled him into the window curtains, then he himself stepped on the favorite corn of a tall Hamlet, and pushed his elbows into a Shylock and broke his false hooked nose, and they both concluded their gyrations by upsetting a couple of brigands, and marching deliberately over the prostrate bodies of Helen McGregor and a matchboy in their progress to a sofa, which they finally reached in an exhausted condition; the lady wanted some water, which Remington started to get but didn't come back, inasmuch as he hurt his shins by tumbling over a chair and fell to the floor, carrying with him in his descent a fairy in one hand and a Fitz James in the other. The crowd immediately closed around him, so that he could not rise, and, as he was involuntarily reposing directly upon the hot air register, he was more than half cooked before he got rescued out.

The attempt to dance created also no small amount of confusion among the others, about twenty-five of whom were precipitated into the conservatory and dispersed through the orchestra. King Lear landed with his head in a French horn, and Byron's Corsair was seen to demolish two violins with his hands at precisely the same time he kicked both feet through the bass drum.

Supper came at last, and the guests were fed in installments, as many getting near the tables as could crowd into the rooms. Jellies, creams, fruits, and the more substantial articles of the repast, were devoured, and scattered over the carpets, and over the dresses of the assembled multitude, in about equal quantities. Champagne corks flew, and all the men of whatever nation, trade, or occupation represented in that incongruous assemblage, seemed to understand perfectly well what champagne was. Kings drank with peasants, brigands touched glasses with monks, and Shylock the Jew took a friendly drink with her majesty the Queen of Sheba.

After supper the smash recommenced, and things grew worse, and the characters, by continued exertion and repeated accidents, became so changed in appearance by the mutilation of their fancy dresses, that at three o'clock in the morning, no one could have picked out any one of the remaining guests and told whether he was intended for an Italian brigand or an Irish washerwoman.

Our friends reached home about daylight, tired, draggled, disgusted, and drunk. Neither of them undressed, but both slept on the floor in the remains of their fancy costume, and in all their paint; they didn't get their faces clean for ten days, but Remington Dropper had seen the Elephant in one of his Fifth Avenue aspects, and was content.

Conclusion.

[Exeunt Omnes.]—Shakespeare.

A few days after the events recorded in the last chapter, a letter was received at the residence of one of the compilers of these records, superscribed

Q. K. PHILANDER DOESTICKS, P. B.

The communication was signed by John Spout, and the writer, after apologizing for communicating with a perfect stranger, stated his reasons for so doing. It seems from the communication that Mr. Spout was informed by a friend who was in the confidence of the United States Marshal, that Mr. Spout and others were accustomed to meet in a room on Broadway, and that they were strongly suspected of being engaged in the organization of a fillibustering expedition to Nicaraugua, and furthermore, that it was the intention of the officious officials of the United States Government to make a descent upon the premises and arrest all who were present on the next regular meeting. Mr. Spout had no difficulty in convincing his friend of the entire misapprehension of the officers. But in the fullness of his modesty the worthy Higholdboy thought that the time was not arrived when it would be prudent to announce to the world the fact of the existence of a scientific association, organized for the purpose of studying the Elephant. Furthermore, he did not like to be arrested, even though he would be acquitted, fearing that contact with stone walls might aggravate a chronic catarrh with which he was afflicted. Under these circumstances, he called a mass meeting of the members of the club, at his private room, where, after a session of fourteen minutes it was unanimously

Resolved, That the Elephant Club cave in for the present, under the pressure of strong necessity.

Resolved, That the landlord of the Club room whistle for the arrearage of rent.

Resolved, That Q. K. Philander Doesticks, P. B., we have every reason to believe, will fully appreciate the high character of the objects of the Elephant Club.

Resolved, That he is hereby authorized to go to the Elephant Club room, secure the records and such other property therein contained, as he may desire.

Resolved, That the said Q. K. Philander Doesticks, P. B., is further authorized to compile the said records for publication, if he thinks the public can be induced to buy the book when it is published; and he is further authorized to reorganize the Club in accordance with the same principles of the old organization, and when the present federal administration goes out of power, the present members will again put on the scientific harness, and gladly co-operate with the club so formed, to secure the ends desired.

In accordance with the request contained, Mr. Doesticks did go to the premises designated, where he found said records, and a variety of articles of furniture in a state of chronic demolition. The records he carried away—the furniture he did not. An examination of the documents satisfied Doesticks that if properly compiled, and published, the work would sell. But feeling himself incompetent to the task of preparation unaided—the work being of a scientific character—he decided to call to his assistance his friend Knight Russ Ockside. In his youth this gentleman had the advantage of being employed in sweeping out the medical college in Thirteenth street, and was once severely injured when young by being hit with a medical book on the head; and these facts it was generally conceded, in accordance with the spirit of modern progression, entitled him to the honorary degree of **M. D.** The scientific part of the work of compilation was therefore left to Dr. Ockside, who has endeavored to do full justice to the subject. Doesticks has reorganized the Elephant Club, and applications for membership will be received by him at No. 70001, Narrow street.

N. B. Applicants will be particular to bring testimonials as to character.

☞ No persons will be received against whom a shadow of suspicion exists that they are of foreign birth, whilst to be a native would be a permanent bar to their membership.

THE END.

DOESTICKS.

DOESTICKS' BOOKS.

12mo, Cloth, per Volume, $1 00.

Among the numerous testimonials from the press in all sections of
the country, we select the following, proving that the author's productions will be sought for and read by thousands of admirers.

NOTICES OF THE PRESS.

"A humorist and a satirist of a very high order. His blows are aimed with
severe accuracy against a vast number of the follies, frailties, and humbugs of
the day."—*Baltimore American, Md.*

"He shows up many of the modern popular humbugs in a very strong light, and
handles them most unmercifully."—*Dayton (Ohio) Daily Empire.*

"Doesticks is a wonder. The same happy spirit seems to pervade the author
and the artist—the illustrations of the latter are quite up to anything Cruikshank
ever achieved in the same line. If anybody can look at these spiritings of the
pencil without a loud laugh, he is certainly out of our list of even grand fellows—
but to enter fully into the pleasing features of the work—to laugh over the jokes,
to enjoy the home-thrusts of wit and satire, our friends must buy the book itself."
—*Sunday Mercury, N. Y.*

"Doesticks is one of the few immortal names that were not born to die. Doesticks will always be with us. We have only to step into our library, and behold
there is the ubiquitous Doesticks! We take him by the hand—we listen to the
thoughts that breathe—the quaint philosophy—the piquant illustration! Doesticks
all over—Doesticks in every page—in every line! Do you wish to make the acquaintance of Doesticks? Every body does."—*New York Railway Journal.*

"The illustrations are in admirable keeping with the general tone of these 'unprecedented extravagances,' and will help to introduce Doesticks and his companions to a large circle of acquaintances."—*McMakin's Philadelphia Saturday
Courier.*

"'Doesticks' is irresistibly funny."—*P. T. Barnum's Letter to the N. Y.
Tribune.*

"Renown has made the euphonious name of 'Doesticks' familiar to the ear of
all the reading public throughout the length and breadth of the land. Those who
would eschew the blues, and drive dull care away, should read Doesticks—what
he says."—*Lansingburg Gazette, N. Y.*

"The 'Doesticks' book is before us. Its inimitable fun sticks to us long after
we have shut the book—its rollicking humor comes back to us in gusts."—*Boston
Chronicle.*

"Doesticks is an original genius. His book is just the thing to pick up at odd
moments, when time hangs heavy, and the mind seeks to be amused."—*Gazette
and Democrat, Reading, Pa.*

"The essays of the rich, racy, humorous, and original Doesticks will be read
by thousands."—*New Orleans Bee.*

"Doesticks' fun is not of the artificial, spasmodic order, it arises from a keen
perception of the humorous side of things."—*New York Tribune.*

"His blows at humbug are trenchant, and his sympathies are ever with humanity."—*Boston Evening Gazette.*

"Doesticks comes to us like a full and sparkling goblet, overflowing with the
rich and brilliant sayings of an original mind. If you would drive away the 'Blue
Devils,' purchase Doesticks, and every sketch you read will be better than any
pill for the indigestion."—*The Uncle Samuel, Boston.*

"What Cruikshanks, Leech, or Gavarni does with the pencil, he accomplishes
with the pen."—*The N. Y. Dutchman.*

"The author is a humorist and a satirist of a very high order. His blows are
aimed with severe accuracy against a vast number of the follies, frailties, and
humbugs of the day,"—*American and Commercial Advertiser, Baltimore, Md.*

LIVERMORE & RUDD, *Publishers,*
310 BROADWAY, NEW YORK.

CPSIA information can be obtained
at www.ICGtesting.com
Printed in the USA
LVHW080846270621
691267LV00008B/388

9 781425 534875